The Art of
CONTAINER
GARDENING

Faith and Geoff Whiten

With paintings by Carol Smith

E. P. DUTTON   NEW YORK

First published 1987, in the United States by
E. P. Dutton

Published in the United States by
E. P. Dutton, a division of New American
Library, 2 Park Avenue New York, N.Y.
10016.

Library of Congress Catalog Number:
86–71941

ISBN: 0-525-24551-0 (Cloth)
ISBN: 0-525-48304-7 (DP)

CUSA

10 9 8 7 6 5 4 3 2 1
First Edition

Designed by Malcolm Harvey Young
Typeset by August Filmsetting, Haydock,
St. Helens
Produced in Portugal by Printer Portuguesa

Contents

1 Why container gardening? 7

2 Containers for gardens 17

3 Planting and care 31

4 Plants 36

5 Sink gardens and ponds in containers 70

6 Planting containers for visual effect 79

7 Where and how to use plants in containers 88

8 Balconies and roof gardens 102

9 Window boxes and wall pots 110

10 Hanging baskets 118

11 Plants for containers 123

Acknowledgements 125

Index 127

Crown imperials in a
decorated earthenware pot.

Chapter one
Why container gardening?

Is it pretentious to call container gardening an art? The process of planting a few geraniums in a pot and placing it by the front door can hardly rate alongside a great painting or literary masterpiece in the field of human inspiration and achievement, and yet gardening in containers demands a certain amount of craft and imagination and offers in return much satisfaction as well as more cheerful and interesting surroundings.

Our use of the word art in the title of this book refers in part to the paintings, drawings and photographs used to illustrate plants in pots and containers and the role that they can play in a garden – or even where a garden hardly exists. Yet we do feel justified in going one step further and describing container gardening itself as an art. Firstly, it is an art in the sense of a craft or skill to persuade a plant to flourish in some sort of container by providing for it the right growing conditions; secondly, it is visual art, for a plant and pot together can create a complete, balanced composition whose shape, colour and texture make it satisfying and interesting to look at.

The art of container gardening is by no means new – people have practised it in different ways and different settings for centuries – and yet today it seems to be one of the most popular forms of gardening, with sales of plant pots, troughs, sinks and boxes – either separately or ready-planted – increasing each year. Why should this be? Well, it is hardly surprising when you consider the way in which we garden as a reflection of the way in which most of us live, for when seen from this viewpoint container gardening has a special appeal and relevance on no fewer than four different levels – the practical, the emotional, the visual and the horticultural.

Why Container Gardening?

First, the practical – one major advantage of growing plants in containers must be that you can do a lot in a very small space; that is surely important as modern gardens seem to be so much smaller, reflecting the ever-increasing cost of land. Many small gardens of both old and new houses are surfaced entirely in paving or even concrete, with no space for plant beds, and so containers are an essential means of introducing plants to soften and brighten what would otherwise be a drab or even dingy environment.

Of course, people who live in flats or other town properties without any garden at all might consider even a paved back yard to be something of a luxury. Yet the practical benefit of containers is that they make gardening possible even in the most apparently impossible situations. A pair of window boxes full of daffodils; a line of hanging baskets trailing red fuchsias; one clipped bay in a wooden tub – any or all of these will fit in the smallest space and can make a tremendous difference to a balcony, a rooftop, a doorstep or the plain brick façade of a house.

So often there seems to be too little time or money available for all the things we want to do, and in both these respects container gardening is a good practical proposition. It does not take long to plant up pots and boxes, and they are then quite easily controllable. Of course, routine maintenance is necessary in the form of watering, feeding and possibly occasional pruning or dead-heading, but this is on a manageable scale and seems to fit easily into one's daily routine when it only takes half an hour or so. In fact, watering can be quite a relaxing and satisfying way of rounding off a summer's evening.

Neither is it necessarily expensive to achieve an impressive effect; pots are a one-off investment and a small quantity of plants goes a long way. A shrub will last for several years and seasonal plants can be grown from seed or bulbs.

When it comes to moving house, it can be a heartbreaking experience to leave behind a mature garden that you have tended and developed as a labour of love over a long period of time. In contrast, the joy of plants in containers is that they can be taken with you. We have moved house on several occasions, and these days find it necessary to organize an extra van into which our treasured collection of plants in pots is packed, wedged and tied with just as much care as the furniture and china! The new house hardly feels like home until we can glance out of the window and get a reassuring glimpse of the hostas in clay flower pots that have multiplied as the plants required splitting; the pine that was grown from a seedling in a Chinese earthenware pot or the conifer that has been tended in that same bowl since about the time our youngest son was born.

Such sentimental attachments lead on to the second level of appeal of container gardening – the emotional. Well, perhaps emotional is too powerful a word. Nobody is likely to be deeply moved to despair or elation by plants in pots but they may be pleased, cheered or delighted by them, and enjoy sharing that pleasure with passers-by – a sentiment that would probably be endorsed by the flower and pot plant salesman in London's Covent Garden market who once reasoned happily, 'We're off to a head's start in this business because everyone loves flowers, don't they?'

A plant in a container can be like a bunch of flowers – bright, showy, frivolous and temporary – or it can be more like a sculpture – full of grace and beauty, with a good shape and strong line that grow and develop over a period of time. In either case, we are likely to respond to its appeal not only because of these qualities but also as part of the natural and instinctive fascination that human beings have always felt towards the living things around them.

It must be said, too, that in a fast-moving world we are drawn in a more impatient, fickle yet entirely understandable way to anything which seems to present possibilities for fast effect. A whole garden can take years to mature, but a container can be planted and positioned in less than a day, and then add to its instant satisfaction by continuing to grow and develop. Container gardening can also satisfy a desire for change and new stimulation. You can quite easily change the pots themselves or the plants that are growing in them, move them around and create a whole new look.

In a sense, container gardening is gardening in miniature and therefore has the appeal of any miniature object or living thing – the fine detail, the neat compactness. This is especially true of, say, a sink garden with dwarf conifers and tiny alpines or a well-shaped

Plants grown in flower pots
were a charming feature of
many Victorian cottage
gardens, as 'The Housewife'
by Frederick Walker
demonstrates.

shrub set amongst rock and pebbles in a shallow bowl, for they represent larger landscape characteristics on a small scale. Just as comparison and imagery seem more resonant than a bald statement of fact, so the small-scale version is somehow more fascinating than the larger original. Anyone can create a rock garden, but how clever to do so in a sink!

This sense of the miniature can also bring out a desire to tend, nurture and care for our container-grown plants like pets, even talking to them and carefully charting their progress with proprietary pride. Just as well, since like pets they are unlikely to thrive in the face of careless neglect and ill treatment!

Quite closely linked to the emotional appeal of plants in containers is their visual appeal. If you are interested in plants and gardens yourself, then you are likely to notice the way in which plants appear and are used around you – sometimes almost without even realizing it consciously. Surely everyone must hold a mental image of even one place or a particular building whose character has been distinguished or even completely dominated by its planted pots, window boxes or hanging baskets. A whole series of pleasant, cheerful and even surprising visual images comes rushing to mind.

The apartment and office blocks of New York would not be quite the same without those threads of trailing green foliage from windows and balconies way up above the streets and a television programme once revealed an unforgettable selection of that city's roof gardens ranging from the quietly sophisticated to the outrageous. In this context, we are reminded of a project undertaken and filmed once by Fisons in an old and dingy series of tenement blocks in a run-down area of London. For just one summer, every balcony and walkway was transformed by Gro-Bags burgeoning with flowers and creating a blaze of cheerful colour. It gave residents a sense of pride in looking good as well as having something good to see.

A drive through London's more prosperous City and West End in springtime is punctuated by a sense of surprise and pleasure at the series of window boxes planted with golden daffodils and variegated ivy in light, jaunty contrast to serious façades in heavy grey stone of banks, embassies and offices. For us, another unforgettable year-round image of London is the frontage of a restaurant in the heart of theatreland, where a row of clipped pyramid bays in pots are chained together on the pavement in neat formation, and ultimately to the building itself, to prevent them from 'walking' – rather like a troop of Roman slaves.

Holland, with its wealth of horticultural produce, is perhaps typified by tubs of tulips and great hanging baskets full of brilliant tuberous begonias. Switzerland in summer is, on the other hand, eternally scarlet geraniums in abundant profusion, contrasting with the neatly ornate, dark-stained timberwork of chalet balconies and shutters. As for Italy, the warmth of summer sunshine floods back as you remember a terraced garden plunging down the hillside, its walls topped with orange trees and oleander in huge terracotta urns.

Whilst those images that are on public view can provide interest and inspiration, most of us are probably more concerned with improving the view from our own back door or front window and the visual impact that can be made by all kinds of plants in all kinds of containers is enormous. A pot on either side of the front door shows you've cared and makes for a more imposing and welcoming entrance; a single window box or hanging basket can make a distinctly architectural contribution, blending with or offsetting the building, and on a more basic level can please simply by matching the curtains in the window.

In a dingy basement or a dull back yard, or on a bare balcony, a little goes a long way, softening and decorating hard surfaces and introducing a natural element to inert surroundings. Planted pots are important as a finishing touch even in the biggest garden, for a paved area is hardly complete without them. They can form a centrepiece or a barrier, a formal sentinel or a happily jumbled group, they can be at ground level or set on a plinth, deck or bench, raising plants so that they are within easy view from the sitting room sofa, dining room table or kitchen sink.

Touching on ideas for the display of pots (which is dealt with later in much more detail) brings us to that fourth level of appeal of

13

Container gardening at
different times and in different
cultures – a gracious country
house in eighteenth century
Europe (painting by Lancret)
and the ancient but surviving
Chinese art of growing a
whole garden in pots (seen
through a moongate at
Tanghua Temple, Kunming).

container gardening – the horticultural – for it presents good opportunities to experiment on quite a small scale, making it ideal both for inexperienced gardeners and those who know and love plants but cannot afford to establish and maintain a large garden. It is also an accessible form of gardening for people whose mental ambition and ideas might otherwise be frustrated by lack of physical strength or mobility. Once positioned and filled with soil, most containers are quite manageable to plant and maintain without the need for constant help from other people or special gadgets.

You can experiment quietly with plants in pots, discreetly hiding any disasters from the world at large but quickly learning from and improving upon them! You can try new plants on a fairly small scale or perhaps invest in just two or three really special plants which have great impact in a pot but would be lost in a garden border. You can, too, be much bolder than many people seem to think, growing not only plants that may not thrive in the prevailing conditions in the garden because they need more shelter or different soil, but also growing quite ambitious plants like climbers, shrubs and small trees. We consider it to be worthwhile to grow a shrub with a beautiful shape in a pot for several years, being prepared that it may eventually reach the end of its useful life or will have to be planted in the garden when it has outgrown its home.

More on that particular subject later, but for the meantime these arguments in favour of practising the art of container gardening – practical, emotional, visual and horticultural – have hopefully prompted a desire for more information and ideas on the various types of containers available, the plants that can be grown in them and the way in which they can be used and displayed in a wealth of different settings.

Chapter two
Containers for gardens

If we are considering container gardening as an art, then it is not enough to gather a random selection of pots with a motley crew of conifers, perennials and leggy geraniums, lump them together in an unswept corner of the patio and fool ourselves that we have created a happily spontaneous and amazingly effective composition. What we will probably have created is quite simply a horrible mess.

Besides, why settle for something jumbled, jarring and completely lacking in impact when for the same effort and expense you could create an absolutely stunning focal point that is an asset to both house and garden as well as winning you gratifying compliments from everyone who sees it? Certainly an informal and varied collection of pots and plants can look good, but only if – like the best apparently casual and haphazard room setting or hairstyle – they are carefully selected and composed so that the styles, colours and shapes all harmonize or contrast happily with each other and their surroundings and the actual arrangement is well shaped and balanced. Then, after perhaps an hour of composition, will the group appear simply to have 'happened' in a clever and appealing way.

As with any artistic composition, it is possible to overdo it when displaying pots in a group and sometimes a single, well-shaped plant in a handsome container would actually be much better, making a dramatic point with a strong outline where both pot and

plant can be fully appreciated. This can apply in an open area, on top of a low wall, at the corner of a patio or the foot of a set of steps – all are points that warrant accentuation which is uncluttered.

Whether they are to be used collectively or individually – as a single feature that has the same impact as a piece of sculpture – both plants and pots will look far better if they are chosen to blend with their eventual setting including the architectural style and period of the house or the character of the garden and the style, colour and finish of the existing materials.

Choosing containers

When it comes to choosing pots, it is also wise to consider the size and type that is most suitable if you want to grow a particular plant, and a material that is practical for its purpose and position in the garden. Visually, size and colour are as important as shape and style. Even if you want the freedom to decide the exact position for a pot when you have got it home, you should at least have an idea of the rough proportions appropriate to the space available. An enormous, ornate stone urn would overpower a tiny back yard, but a couple of small flowerpots would be lost at the far end of a long path.

Having mentioned these points to bear in mind, it should be said that the choice of pot need not be a dull business full of restrictions and dire warnings of unsuitability. Choosing a container should actually be one of the great pleasures of container gardening, especially if like us you have a weakness for beautiful and unusual china and wooden objects indoors. This seems to transfer quite comfortably to an irresistible desire to fill the garden with pots that have a beautiful shape, an appealing surface or fascinating decorative details.

Fortunately, the increased popularity of container gardening has led to pots being available in a wide range of materials to suit just about all tastes and pockets.

As might be expected, the most economical pots to buy are not the most glamorous but they are practical. Planters made from natural cellular fibre come in the shape of long, narrow troughs as well as

Well-composed group for a
shady corner includes foxgloves, astilbe, hostas and fern.

round, square and hexagonal designs; they have an earthy colour and knobbly texture that might not suit all tastes but they do provide excellent growing conditions for plants because the fibre breathes. They are intended to be for temporary use, lasting a couple of years, after which the fibre is bio-degradable.

These inexpensive pots are ideal if you want to fill a sunny yard or balcony with colour on a budget; they could be positioned in informal groups of five or seven containing seasonal flowers – fuchsias, geraniums, petunias and silver-leaf – or even vegetables – tomatoes, peppers, aubergines.

Plastic may be a more durable material, but in our opinion it often fails to blend easily with plants and natural surroundings. Modern designs with a clean, simple line succeed best; plastic is, after all, a modern material and of course comes in almost any colour. Geometrically shaped plastic pots in bright, primary colours containing white flowers (petunias, geraniums, tulips) and foliage plants like chlorophytum (the little spider plant), coleus and silver-leaf annuals could look jauntily cheerful on a sunny balcony or in a small, modern patio garden where they might be matched with brightly coloured garden furniture.

From a horticultural point of view, plastic pots are best for short-term plants because the material does not breathe. If you want something fairly simple in which plants may be more likely to thrive in the long term, then ordinary clay flower pots would be an excellent choice. The smaller sizes are usually machine-made and therefore low in price and they can be displayed in groups to great effect – perhaps with saucers to give them more presence. Half-pots, too, are extremely useful for plants like geraniums, pot marigolds, polyanthus and petunias for their wider, shallow form makes for a more balanced composition. The plants can spill nicely over the edges and the whole thing does not appear to be bottom heavy as sometimes happens when full pots are used. They are useful, too, for azaleas and all plants that need only a shallow root depth.

Machine-made clay pots may be handy and inexpensive, but their more sophisticated relatives – handmade terracotta in ornate or traditionally simple designs – are among the most useful and versatile garden containers. The material has a smooth, warm texture; it is a pleasant, earthy colour that blends into so many settings, and being porous it allows soil to drain well and roots to breathe. It is also suitable for a wide range of plants including shrubs, perennials, bulbs, annuals, herbs and even vegetables.

Although the character and feel of terracotta is associated with sunny climates like the southern Mediterranean or California, pots, urns and troughs can be visually versatile, blending well into many settings from a plain new house or modern apartment block to more ornate Colonial, Georgian and Victorian buildings, and with many architectural materials. Obviously pots look especially well with red brick, but they can also sit happily with stone, timber and even concrete, and the many designs available make it simpler to choose one which is most appropriate to the prevailing period and character.

A practical word of caution is necessary here, because by no means all terracotta pots are tolerant of frost. This is especially true of those made in areas where the weather is temperate all year round, so do check when buying if you live in an area where the temperature normally falls below freezing in winter as pots may crack and even burst in these conditions. It is possible, however, to buy frost-proof terracotta pots, often with a guarantee against frost damage.

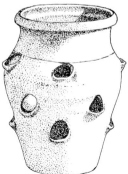

21

Glazed earthenware pots from China may look exotic, but they are in fact extremely robust and weatherproof. The major range now available in the West are traditional high-fired earthenware planters from the Ihsing pottery, which is situated in Jiangsu province in central China, and has been established for many hundreds of years. In fact, London's Victoria & Albert museum displays Ihsing planters that date back to the sixteenth century and yet are similar to those still made today. Chinese potters, it seems, see no need to pander to the passing whims of trends and high fashion!

We should be glad of their adherence to tradition, for it means that we can now grow plants in our own gardens in fluted Ihsing pots finished in the beautiful mottled dark blue glaze known as 'Chun' meaning 'sky after rain'. In a mixture of subtle greens, browns and yellows other pots bear ornate oriental decoration featuring flowers, leaves, birds, butterflies, pandas and fierce, swirling dragons. Shapes range from shallow round, hexagonal and square pots with saucers to enormous egg pots and a dramatic 'body jar', the latter being an imposing ornamental object in its own right. It could form an effective focal point in association with smaller pots that would actually be planted. Egg pots are finished inside in a turquoise shade, and look equally good filled with water and one or two floating plants to make a pond in a pot.

Larger Chinese earthenware pots are not cheap, but they are a good long-term investment and capable of giving a lift to any patio or front door area. The natural colours help them – like terracotta – to blend in many settings, but especially where decoration is called for or, of course, if the garden already has an oriental 'feel'. They are useful, too, for larger, long-term plants like a small tree, a shrub or a climber and also for stunning colour combinations – perhaps a blue or white hydrangea or a bluish-grey pine in a blue pot and in the decorated pots plants with gold or orange flowers like narcissus, crown imperials or lilies.

22

Imposing marble pot
containing bamboo.

Containers for Gardens

Of course not all beautiful earthenware pots come from China, and if you come across a fairly large pot that is really special, it could look just as good in the garden or on the balcony as indoors. Even a lovely jardiniere (or indeed any pot) that is not frostproof can spend the warmer months of the year in the garden and the colder ones in the house. If you have a conservatory, where pots can be over-wintered, the possibilities are even greater as long as the containers can be moved fairly easily.

Another excellent material for containers in which trees or shrubs are to be planted – or indeed any other type of plant – is wood. Round wooden tubs with metal hoops are simple and traditional; they can be varnished so that the natural grain is enhanced or stained or painted. Green is the most common shade, and a fairly neutral, olive green blends more happily with most plants than fierce emerald shades. Versailles tubs are more formal but equally traditional and whilst they are commonly finished in natural wood or white paint, this style of tub could in theory be finished in any colour that would match an existing scheme.

Plain tubs and troughs in more modern designs look good with slatted timber paving or decking, where they are effective containing uniform plants and positioned in a straight line along one edge of the deck or paved area. Many new houses have doors and windows finished in wood preservative rather than paint and tubs could be treated in the same shade to blend effectively, uniting house and garden. However, plant containers are best finished in a water-based stain or preservative rather than creosote, which can be harmful to plants.

Stone containers – whether 'real' or made from reconstituted stone – have a feel of solid permanence. Some are made in simple,

Square wooden tubs with
slatted timber paving.

modern designs and finished in various subtle colour effects; this makes them quite informal and appropriate for modern gardens and small spaces although their weight hardly lends them to being moved around at whim! Other stone containers are much more traditional or even classical in design; some are actual reproductions of antique urns and pots situated in the gardens of the stately homes, castles and palaces of Europe.

Such distinguished origins give a clue to the most appropriate setting for their use; it is important to use such ornate, stately and often rather large pieces in a garden that is equally large and imposing. Of course it is not necessary to have rolling acres; a single ornate urn planted with a hydrangea or rhododendron can make a superb focal point for a patio or terrace of, say 20 ft (6 m) square or the centrepiece of a formal basement garden. A pair would look equally imposing on either side of a porticoed front door with steps leading up to it; the architecture can take it.

In smaller gardens, back yards and balconies it is perhaps better to choose a stone pot that is quite small and fairly simple, making it lighter in both weight and appearance and therefore more suited to the surroundings. Such a pot allows greater flexibility of planting, too, for a really large, pretentious stone urn or trough demands bold plants that balance, which probably means conifers or 'choice' shrubs with glossy leaves or large flowers. Summer bedding plants are rather light and delicate in appearance to create a comfortable composition in large urns, but they can look superb in a smaller, simpler stone pot.

Other containers with a rather aristocratic feel are those made in lead and marble. Rather like stone, they can look good in the right setting and quite silly or downright disastrous in the wrong one. Both would go well with white painted walls or blue brick and with paving in grey shades – especially natural slate or York stone. They are also well suited to being associated with water, having a smooth surface, but marble especially is not well suited to rustic brick or rugged, informal stone.

Pots of polyanthus in a simple
tray on the window sill.

Containers for Gardens

Although these are just some of the containers available from stores and garden centres, it is equally possible to improvise, making your own planters or recycling something that was originally intended for quite a different purpose. Of course, in theory anything that is more or less watertight and has drainage holes in the bottom can be used as a receptacle in which to grow plants – and that includes plastic buckets and painted paint tins. It could also include objects that will hold a plant already growing in a rigid plastic or clay flower pot – objects such as old chimney pots, which are still available as reclaimed items and even as newly manufactured reproductions.

Chimney pots, with their distinctly Victorian and Edwardian flavour, look well in the garden of a house of the same period, especially if combined with other furniture and fittings in the same style. We once worked on a project with *Practical Householder* magazine which combined chimney pots with a table made from the base of an old treadle sewing machine, a garden storage cupboard that had once been a large, ornate wardrobe and a bridge hand-rail made from a Victorian bedhead – both the latter being finished in glossy black laquer.

There seems to be almost no end to the possibilities for quirky and humorous invention of plant containers recycled from objects designed for a different purpose entirely. A gardening magazine once had quite an amazing response to a competition for such inventions, with entries (in which plants were actually grown) ranging from lavatory pans and chamber pots to coal scuttles, kettles and wheelbarrows. Not necessarily elegant, but novel nonetheless!

Pink camellia in a decorated
lead container.

Chapter three
Planting and care

Container gardening is the art of persuading plants to flourish in what is for them a totally artificial environment. In good open ground, plants take their nourishment from the soil and their moisture requirement from the rain, but in containers they are totally dependent for their existence on the conditions provided for them initially, and on the quality and consistency of care and attention devoted to them subsequently. It is therefore important to meet their four basic needs, which are fortunately quite simple. At the time of planting they are for adequate drainage and a suitable growing medium and, on a long term basis, for regular watering and feeding.

Firstly, drainage, and whatever the type of container, it should have adequate holes in the bottom to allow excess water to drain freely. You may also need to raise the base of the pot so that it is slightly off the ground to ensure that water runs away – although this should not be necessary if the pot is standing on a base of shingle gravel or some other aggregate which is itself a free-draining material. To prevent the drainage holes becoming clogged, a layer of crocks from broken clay flower pots should be placed in the bottom before compost is added. If these are not available you could use pebbles or fired grandules of clay or cinterized ash of about $\frac{1}{2}$ in (13 mm) diameter. Whatever you use, it is a good idea to place on top a few pieces of well-rotted turf or a layer of coarse peat.

When it comes to the actual growing medium, ordinary soil from the garden definitely will not do. Instead, it is necessary to use a potting compost and here you can choose between peat-based compost, loam-based compost or one which combines the two. Each has its advantages and advocates, but the choice is ultimately a personal one depending on your preference and requirements.

Peat-based compost is light in weight, so it would be an advantage in containers that might be moved around a lot. It is also a good, airy medium for roots but it does not hold much food value and no trace elements (vital minerals normally present in soil). It also tends to dry out quickly and indeed, if you allow a peat-based compost to dry out completely, plants may suffer irreparable damage.

John Innes is a loam-based compost made to a certain formula rather than a commercial brand. It has more food value and better moisture retention than peat, and it does contain trace elements, but it also weighs more heavily. There are three grades and in containers No. 2 would suit annuals, vegetables and so on but No. 3 is the best all-purpose choice for permanent and long-term plants. Ericaceous plants like rhododendrons, azaleas and camellias need an acid soil and therefore a specially prepared mix. Ask for an ericaceous or rhododendron mix peat-based compost or – for a loam-based compost – John Innes No. 3 without chalk.

In Britain (as one might expect perhaps!) there is a compromise choice for compost – a Universal compost mix which consists of a John Innes type with added peat, making it open, airy and rather lighter in weight.

Whatever the choice of compost, when planting take care to disturb the roots of plants as little as possible. If you buy them grown in pots from the nursery or garden centre, then they should transplant quite happily and settle quickly. Remove the growing container carefully and gently fan out any roots at the base of the soil and root ball. Water the container as soon as the plant is firmed in; give it a good quantity of water each time subsequently, so that you can see it draining through the holes in the bottom of the pot.

Finally, you could spread a layer of ornamental gravel or shingle on the soil surface around a shrub or tree in a container; this will help to conserve moisture and keep the plant's roots cool and will help to prevent the surface of the soil from being washed away when you water.

As for frequency of watering, this is inevitably to some extent a question of judgement based on the needs that arise from the type of plant and its position, the type of compost and the material of the container. However, we find that it is best to water container plants morning and evening in spring and summer; at least once a day is certainly a general rule. A large specimen growing in full sun in the summer may also need to be watered again around midday, but you should take care not to wet the foliage. On the other hand, for plants like hostas and ferns growing in a damp shady place twice a day would be too much.

In winter there is not a great deal to do with container plants, but it is as well to be aware of the danger that during a prolonged period of frost and ice, the compost and roots may become freeze dried. When a thaw eventually sets in, do check containers for this and if added moisture is necessary wait for a mild period (two or three days is enough) before watering gently. Never water when there is the possibility that the container will refreeze, even overnight.

Watering can be a time consuming job, especially if you choose to use a watering can as we do, rather than a hose pipe. Do remember that the more containers you have, the more work is involved although we find that this can become quite absorbing and even relaxing. It is possible to minimize the time that watering demands by grouping containers together in certain parts of the garden rather than placing the odd one or two in numerous different locations.

Feeding is also necessary during the growing season. If you use a can to water, it is easy enough to add a measure of general liquid fertilizer whilst filling the can at the tap. We feed container plants about once a week, again using judgement and feeding even more frequently any plant that looks a little sickly. Do remember to water the container before feeding, because if you pour diluted fertilizer on to dry soil it will simply wash through without having a chance to be effective.

In spring it is a good idea to fork out gently the top inch or so of compost in the containers of long-term plants. Tease up the new surface and then add a layer of fresh, new compost. You could also add a sprinkling of bone meal or granular general fertilizer at the same time, as an extra feed. Indeed, there are other ways of applying

33

A well-shaped rhododendron
in blue glazed earthenware pot

fertilizer to container plants – even a pellet which can be placed just under the soil surface to give slow-release fertilizer and weedkiller combined. On the subject of weeds, these should obviously be removed from containers as soon as they appear – a job that only takes a minute or two.

Even when container plants are established you may still want to move them around the garden from time to time – that is, after all, part of the ever-changing interest of container gardening. For this job, we find it essential to have on hand a low, flat trolley on wheels or castors. The pot can be eased up on to the trolley using a spade as a lever.

In spring our trolley is in constant use, bringing hostas out of winter hibernation or moving the specimen *Acer palmatum dissectum* into the sun. This is a beautiful, mature plant in a heavy pot and early in the season as the delicate foliage starts to break we tend to leave it on the trolley so that it can quickly and easily be moved in response to weather conditions. We are anxious to avoid burning by the sudden warm spring sunshine or damage from a sharp east wind; as already mentioned, acer leaves can be delicate and when the plant is finally placed in its position for the summer, brown specks would spoil the whole look of that lovely foliage effect.

Chapter four
Plants

Shape and Outline

Just as choosing the right containers for your patio, balcony, basement or wherever should be a pleasurable experience, so deciding on which plants to grow in containers can be interesting and even exciting, especially since the options are so varied. We have all seen pots bursting with geraniums or bearing a single column-shaped conifer that hardly changes its appearance all through the year, and whilst each can be very successful they are perhaps rather well-worn images.

It is certainly possible to be more adventurous, since there are many plants of all types and sizes that lend themselves very well to container gardening whether in sunshine or shade, on a grand or

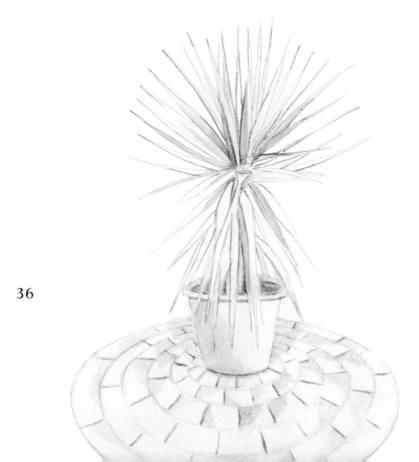

small scale, on a permanent or temporary basis. However, just because it is horticulturally possible for a plant to flourish in a container does not, as far as we are concerned, automatically qualify it for recommendation. After all, we are considering container gardening as an art, not a horticultural exercise alone. We believe that the visual aspect of container gardening is absolutely vital – that planted containers are a design feature of the area in which they are placed, however small that may be.

The composition of pot and plant or plants together is going to take the form of a complete ornamental feature in its own right – one that will probably be seen from many angles – and therefore shape and balance are two vital bye-words. Some simple guidelines on what constitutes good shape and a well-balanced composition are given later, but it is essential to emphasize their importance before moving on to talk specifically about plants that you might choose to grow.

What does make a good container plant? Naturally our recommendations are personal ones, but having said that shape is important, perhaps we should define this more precisely. Good container plants should have a distinctive outline that demands to be viewed from all directions away from other plants – whether that is neatly symmetrical or a strikingly random shape that nevertheless has a pleasing, well-balanced line. So, shrubs that are distinguished by a strong architectural shape like cordyline, or tend by natural habit to form a dense, rounded plant like a rhododendron or hydrangea are ideal – as are those plants which whilst dense, have drooping habit so that they fall gracefully over the edges of the pot. Some phormiums and most fuchsias are examples.

Look at the structure of the plant; the most successful in containers are either nearly perfect specimens of their type or, in the case of some conifers especially, those that have gone towards the other extreme and grown away from type, giving them an asymmetrical shape that is full of interest and character.

Shape is not only concerned with the outline of the plant, but with its actual form – the way in which the leaves grow almost in layers in lush foliage plants like hostas or the twisted twigs of

37

corkscrew hazel, which is especially effective when interlaced by its drooping catkins adding yet another dimension. Flowers, too, might be capable of forming a bold mass like tulips or narcissus, their stems neatly upright. Other flowering plants are striking for the shape and colour of the bloom itself; lilies and crown imperials are just two examples.

The third aspect of container plants that is closely associated with shape and form is detail. Details such as leaf shape and texture, variegation, flower form and colour can all help to make a plant special – as with delicately variegated ivy or the large rich, glossy leaves of *Fatsia japonica*. However, they are features which tend to be noticed more at close quarters and most container plants make their initial impact from a distance – however short – so details should be used to enhance shape and outline rather than to replace them, and this is especially true of permanent plants as opposed to those grown seasonally in containers.

Trees

Perhaps the largest of all the permanent plants that you might try growing in a container are trees. The idea may be rather more ambitious than you had contemplated, but if you have a yard with no plant beds or a basement garden – even a large, open patio – height is important. It can be achieved with climbers around walls and on fences but in an open position a small, graceful tree makes a superb centrepiece.

Before discussing some of the most suitable trees it is important to make a practical point. All small trees or large shrubs grown in containers will thrive for several years if the pot is sufficiently large and they are kept well fed and watered. However, they should be regarded only as semi-permanent because in time (perhaps after four to five years) the tree or shrub may become root-bound. Then you should remove it carefully from the pot and plant it either in a suitable position in your own garden or – if you have no space or no plant beds – why not donate it to a friend or relative?

Dramatic outlines and
shadows; cordylines in clay
pots on circular block paving
at Mrs Winthrop's garden,
Hidcote.

You can usually tell when a tree is starting to become pot-bound; when the leaves appear they may be smaller than normal and the plant generally looks less thriving than it did – perhaps even a little sickly. Planting into open ground is best carried out between autumn and very early spring, and the tree should not be too difficult to remove from the container since there will be a mass of root and little soil. Dig a generous hole to receive the roots, adding peat and fertilizer to the soil; before planting remove any crocks that may be attached to the bottom of the tree's roots and gently unravel the ends, fanning them outwards a little to encourage them to spread naturally in the soil, having become accustomed to the confined conditions of the container.

One final piece of advice: the joys of container gardening are such that when you have done this you can go and browse around the nursery or garden centre, select a different tree – and start all over again!

Small weeping trees

The best small trees for containers in our view are those with a weeping shape. Their structure means that there is little bare trunk between container and branches; rather, they fall back down towards the container, making a pleasing composition. In winter, the shape of the bare branches and their gracefully weeping line are still attractive, making them good all year round plants. They are also quite easy to manage as the branches are accessible and can therefore be trimmed and pruned to perfect shape as necessary. A word of warning, however – pruning in this way should be a delicate operation, not major surgery. Do it in the dormant period using good quality, sharp secateurs and just trim sparingly the odd side shoot that spoils the overall symmetry or line of the plant – those twigs that suddenly branch off at an uncomfortable angle.

As for varieties, one of the neatest and most compact weeping trees is the Kilmarnock willow *Salix caprea* 'Pendula'. The whole tree grows to little more than 8 ft (2.5 m) tall, producing greater density of branches as it matures. These weep rather stiffly, creating an umbrella shaped tree that is equally appealing for its bare stems in winter, its 'pussy willow' catkins in spring and its mass of quite large leaves in summer. Because of the obvious association between willow trees and water, this might look good positioned close to a garden pond.

If foliage interest is important to you, then an equally good choice would be the little weeping purple beech, *Fagus sylvatica* 'Purpurea Pendula'. Its large leaves are green on one side and dark purple on the other whilst the tree itself, like the Kilmarnock willow, is quite miniature in size with stiff branches that spread outwards before they weep strongly, rather creating the overall effect of a toadstool on a stem. Somewhat larger and taller in habit, but with equally beautiful foliage is Young's weeping birch, *Betula pendula* 'Youngii'. It has the characteristically small, rustling leaves and soft, swaying branches of silver birch – branches that weep right down to the ground – and the added appeal of the familiar silvery-white bark.

If you are looking for a container tree that will bring winter interest to the garden, but prefer not to go for a conifer, then there are two small weeping trees which would be ideal the first is *Cotoneaster* 'Hybridus Pendulus', which is in fact an evergreen cotoneaster shrub grafted on to an erect, standard stem. The branches weep

Salix caprea 'Pendula'.

Bamboo grown in bonsai
fashion makes a distinctive
specimen plant.

Mature specimen of *Acer palmatum* 'Dissectum' with fine, delicate foliage and a beautiful overall shape that has been carefully encouraged for several years.

The intriguing corkscrew hazel (*Corylus avellana* 'Contorta') is centrepiece of a pleasing group. It is complemented by pots planted simply with pinks and ivy.

rather stiffly and from autumn through into the winter months are covered in clusters of brilliant red berries. Holly too is quite well suited to container growing because it is so slow, and the weeping *Ilex aquifolium* 'Pendula' not only has rich, dark green spiny leaves but also usually bears a profusion of red berries.

If yours is a tiny urban garden with wall-to-wall concrete or paving, then you will probably appreciate container plants that flower early in the year just to remind you that spring occurs in town as well as in the country! The ornamental flowering cherry *Prunus* 'Cheal's Weeping' is an excellent small specimen tree which has branches that weep quite stiffly and steeply. In April the pale green leaves are offset by clusters of pink buds which open to double flowers of rose pink – a soft, frothy confection of blossom that might go well with tubs of white tulips or shallow clay pans of blue scilla or muscari.

Other small trees and large shrubs

A number of excellent plants lend themselves to container gardening in the same way as weeping trees. Good to grow as specimens in an open position, their classification tends to blur between small tree or large shrub. Perhaps the most novel is a bush apple or plum tree, developed by grafting on to really dwarf rootstock. These are available from specialist fruit growers and make ideal container plants even in the longer term, for they remain no larger than a good-sized shrub.

Of much more exotic appearance is the Japanese angelica tree, *Aralia elata*. In winter its main stem is quite unremarkable, but as the leaves break a dramatic transformation takes place for this tiny tree produces enormous, spreading leaves that can reach up to 3 ft (1 m) long. Each leaf is divided into a regular series of 'leaflets' and towards the end of the summer the top of the tree is covered in frothy white flowers. Although *Aralia elata* is hardy in temperatures as low as approximately minus 35°F, it thrives best in a position sheltered from cold draughts. Both the ordinary elata and two variegated forms make bold plants that are real eye-catchers.

A shrub that may also be considered quite unusual for a container, but is nevertheless a very worthy candidate, is the corkscrew hazel *Corylus avellana* 'Contorta' (also known as Harry Lauder's walking stick). As the name suggests, both branches and twigs are quite tortuously twisted, making a really striking plant. In winter the bare stems alone are fascinating; in early spring they are punctuated by streamers of long yellow catkins and in summer rich green leaves slowly unfurl to cover the plant. In the open ground corkscrew hazel grows to about 9 ft (3 m) tall, but in a container it grows slowly and in our experience remains quite dwarfed for several years.

One of our favourite groups of shrubs for container gardening is the Japanese maple, *Acer palmatum* and its close relatives. Here is a plant that can grow into most beautiful irregular shapes, making a graceful specimen that, together with its pot, really deserves the description of sculpture – a plant with a truly oriental feel. Like corylus, the bare winter twigs alone are graceful when the plant has established its form, but the leaves are the real feature, both in summer and in autumn when they turn fiery shades of yellow, red and orange.

All varieties of *Acer palmatum* are slow growing, so they can be grown in a container for many years, and can be trimmed to encourage them to form the best possible shape, perhaps following their inclination to lean to one side. They like a peaty soil and the leaves can be quite delicate so are best sheltered from both wind and late frosts. *Acer palmatum* 'Atropurpureum' has deeply divided leaves of dark bronzy-purple, whilst *A. palmatum* 'Dissectum' has leaves which are much more finely cut and are a fresh, delicate shade of slightly yellowish green. *A. palmatum* 'Dissectum Atropurpureum' has dark purple leaves which are similarly finely toothed.

Although acers are sculptural they are plants with a soft, flowing shape and light stems which move in the breeze, the leaves creating a rippling effect. This, together with their tendency to lean, makes them ideal plants to grow in a pot beside a pond.

Equally sculptural but in a more rigid and formal way is the bay tree, *Laurus nobilis*. The stiff, leathery, dark green leaves are well

The simplicity of blue
hydrangeas in a square pot
has considerable impact beside
this front door.

Pink hydrangeas soften the
corner of a pool. The clay pot
blends with bricks and a rich
crimson rhododendron makes
a bold backdrop.

Stunning azaleas in a potted
landscape garden at the
Garden of the Humble
Administrator, Suzhou, China.

known for their aromatic character making the plant useful for culinary purposes as well as for its ornamental quality. As an evergreen container plant it usefulness lies both in the various clipped shapes available – from lower growing pyramid to a ball head on standard stem – and in its ability to lend an air of sophisticated smartness to its surroundings. Ideal in pairs or even larger formal groupings such as a straight line to form a demarcation, perhaps in a courtyard or at the edge of a formal patio, bay trees look good in stone pots, wooden tubs or ornamental terracotta designs, the latter emphasizing their Mediterranean origin.

This origin means that bay trees are best protected from frost, being particularly susceptible to damage in cold, inland regions. They are quite slow growing and therefore take some time to mature as specimens – this being reflected in their price which is usually rather high. They are easy to keep in shape by gentle trimming of any leaves that threaten to spoil the overall outline.

A similarly slow-growing evergreen with dense, luxuriant foliage is box, *Buxus sempervirens*. As a British native plant it is more hardy than bay, but is very slow growing, so specimen container plants tend to be quite small pyramids, and are increasingly seen in the form of topiary – traditional shapes of birds and the like. Neat, round bush specimens are particularly effective when grown in a uniform row, each in the same style of pot, creating something akin to a low, formal hedge. The uniform dark green foliage looks well in decorated earthenware pots – perhaps in traditional oriental blue and white designs if you can find them – or in small, square, white painted wooden tubs.

Shrubs

Although there are a number of shrubs which could be grown in containers we are, as mentioned, concentrating on those that are particularly valuable for their shape and structure. However, this by no means rules out shrubs which have appealing foliage and flowers, for some of the most useful are also among the most beautiful when in bloom.

Two choice evergreen shrubs which have good foliage and out-
standing flowers are rhododendron and camellia. Both are ericaceous plants, so they will need suitable compost and maintenance, as mentioned previously in our advice for planting and care.
Rhododendrons flower in late spring–early summer and the numerous hybrids offer a wealth of colour from white, palest yellow, pink
or lavender through to hot red, deep crimson or rich purple. Whilst
the lighter shades would be complemented by a green wooden tub
or a dark blue or decorated greeny-brown glazed earthenware container, the rich, deep flower colours would – like the plant's dark
leaves – contrast well with a grey or buff stone pot.

Low to medium growing varieties are best for containers – those
that normally grow to no more than about 4 ft (1.25 m) – and when
you are choosing a plant look for a nice shape, whether well
rounded or slightly irregular. A dense plant with close, compact
habit is better than one with very open branches. As for position,
rhododendrons prefer partial shade and should be placed away from
strong winds. A plant in a pot or urn makes an ideal single specimen, but if you want to place it together with other containers, then
bulb flowers go well, as do fuchsias and trailing variegated ivy. You
could even grow it in close proximity to a camellia.

Dwarf conifers in decorated
oriental pots make an effective
formal feature on a bed or
raised bench of gravel.

Camellias are exotic-looking plants whose Chinese origin seems somehow obvious from the high gloss of the leaves to the perfection of the single or double flowers. Again, numerous named hybrids are available but all require careful cultivation – or at least correct conditions, which means partial shade (damp shade is so much the better) and protection from frost, for the roots must never become frozen through or the plant will die. Plants can survive where the temperature does not fall below 12°F (-11°C) but in any event the pot must be insulated with bracken, straw, sawdust or similar material from autumn right through the winter in order to protect the roots. Where feeding is concerned, this should be carried out between April and July only.

Two splendid and less fussy flowering plants for containers are hydrangeas and roses. The rounded shape of hydrangeas and their long-lasting flowers – large, showy and flamboyant – make them ideal where a bold effect is required, especially together with rather heavy stonework against which small, dainty plants would be lost. The mophead types are probably most familiar, but lacecaps are perhaps even more appealing with flatter blooms which have a softer, lacy appearance.

The colour of hydrangea flowers varies according to the soil. One rich in lime produces red or pink flowers, but in acid soil the flowers are blue, and you could encourage this by adding blueing powder every week or two during the growing season. Remove the dead flowers of lacecaps in autumn, but leave mopheads until the following March before removing.

Roses need no introduction. In containers they are easy to grow, thriving in a sunny place and flowering throughout the summer. Climbing roses are considered separately, but as bushes it is best to grow in pots either modern shrub roses that are fairly compact in habit or a hybrid tea or floribunda with a nice shrubby shape that will not become too leggy. The choice of varieties and colours is enormous, and neither should miniatures and ground cover types be forgotten. These are especially effective massed in a bowl-shaped planter or a long trough.

Wisteria around the front door.

From flowers to foliage, and a random group of foliage plants which have in common a splendid architectural shape, giving them true sculptural quality. First *Fatsia japonica* whose large, glossy, fig-like leaves give it a lush appearance. This plant tolerates town conditions and blends well with urban architecture; it likes some shelter and will grow in shade, so would be a good choice for containers in a basement garden or north facing balcony. A nice bold plant for a corner or in a wall niche as well as a more open situation.

Yucca and cordyline both have a Mediterranean look and prefer a warm, sunny position, where either makes a magnificent centre-piece. Both have strong, spear-like foliage and yucca also throws up magnificent white panicles of flowers on long stems in late summer. They look good in rather bulbous terracotta pots – either plain or decorated – which seem to complement their shape.

Two natives of New Zealand have a similarly spiky shape and are similarly intolerant of very cold, damp conditions. Insulation of the base of the plant with straw or bracken is advisable in areas where temperatures regularly fall below freezing.

The first is astelia, which has leaves like silver swords with a matt, distinctly silvery surface and is capable of lifting and lightening a dark surface such as old brickwork. A couple of pots of red geraniums nearby would complete the composition.

The New Zealand flax, *Phormium tenax*, has long, stiff spears and can grow up to 6 or 7 ft (2 m) tall but there are several named varieties, some of which are more drooping in their habit, more compact in size and very appealing for their colour. *P. tenax* 'Sundowner' has wide leaves with a greyish purple midriff and creamy pink outer band, and *P. tenax* 'Yellow Wave' has golden yellow leaves with green outer edges.

Golden variegation is a characteristic of one final architectural plant which does not qualify as a shrub but is nevertheless permanent. *Arundinaria viridistriata* is a small bamboo with lovely bright colouring but a fairly dwarf habit, reaching no more than 4 ft (1.2 m) tall, and could be grown as a clump in quite a small container.

Conifers

Conifers come in all shapes and sizes and for container gardening they are useful as year-round permanent plants – especially those which are by nature dwarf or slow growing and will therefore thrive in a pot for many years. A slow-growing conifer is not necessarily tiny, and two taller specimens are especially useful where an upright plant is needed for height and accent. *Juniperus virginiana* 'Skyrocket' makes a narrow, pencil-shaped column of blue-grey foliage which retains its shape well and *Thuja occidentalis* 'Smaragd' forms a pyramid of fresh, bright green which eventually reaches about 8 ft (2.5 m) over quite a long period of time.

If you do want a really dwarf conifer with an attractive shape, then a good choice would be *Picea glauca* 'Albertiana Conica' – a large name for a small spruce (up to about 3 ft (1 m) tall) which is

neatly conical and in spring looks a real treat, covered in the fresh season's growing tips of bright green. Varieties of the mountain pine, *Pinus mugo* – 'Humpy', 'Mops' and 'Ophir' for example – are also neat, small and slow growing but have the slightly wilder, looser look typical of pine and are therefore less formal. They would go well in a small wooden tub of natural varnished wood or in a wide, shallow trough or bowl with the soil surface covered in stone chippings and larger pebbles to make a miniature landscape.

There is nothing at all miniature about *Cedrus deodara* and *Cedrus atlantica glauca*, for both are notable cedar trees which can grow to really enormous height and spread – not the size of plant one might normally choose to grow in a pot. However, we have a specimen of each in our own garden, both of which have been growing in containers for several years. They have almost taken on the characteristics of a bonsai plant, forming shapes that lean to one side in an appealing way. Naturally they have to be fed well and trimmed to shape occasionally, and once settled in a position where they thrive, do not respond well to being moved. However, if you are willing to invest care and attention in really handsome conifers like these, then you will be rewarded by a container plant that is unusual – even unique – and a joy to look at and watch over as it develops, almost like a pet.

Climbing plants

What do you do to soften and brighten up a basement garden or back yard that is surfaced in paving or concrete and surrounded by walls or fences? The first inclination of any gardener is to grow climbing plants to soften and clothe those hard boundaries, and if there is no possibility of making plant beds at ground level, then you might create raised beds – or you must grow the all-important climbers in containers. The same solution applies if your patio goes right up to the garden boundary making an unbroken meeting of horizontal and vertical hard surfaces, or if a pergola shelters a paved area and there is no space at the base of the timber uprights for soil in which can be planted climbers that twine and scramble upwards.

Clematis in a stone bowl with
pebbles.

Similarly, if you want to create a plant-clad screen to hide a utility area or establish a divide between hard surfaced areas of different character, then trellis panels and a couple of climbing plants in pots may just do the trick.

Permanent climbers need much the same treatment as shrubs when growing in containers, and it is especially important to plant them in a pot that is reasonably large and sufficiently substantial to support the plant over a long period of time, as well as paying careful attention to feeding. Also, do position the plant in a place where it is likely to thrive. There are two ways of approaching this; either you will decide that you simply must have, say , a wisteria, and then look around for a sunny place in which to settle it or you might feel that a dull, north-facing wall desperately needs softening, and then find for that purpose say an ivy or a *Clematis montana*.

Both ivy and clematis are good for container gardening. Both offer a wide choice of varieties for all sites and situations and are easy to grow; they can clothe walls, fences, trellis, pergolas, tree trunks and can cascade downwards as well as climbing upward. This is especially true of ivy, so you could grow it in a container positioned on top of a wall or on a pedestal, allowing the foliage to tumble and twine informally.

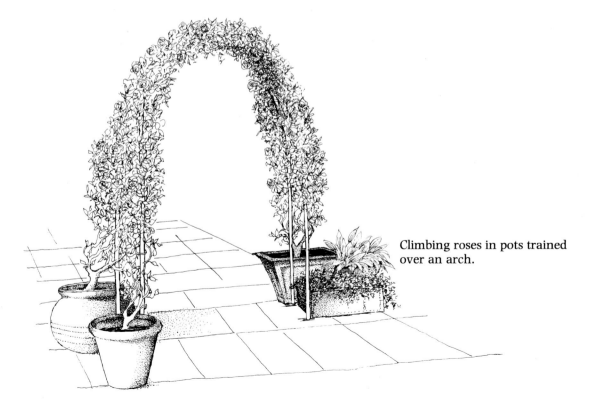

Climbing roses in pots trained over an arch.

Wisteria is a favourite with almost everyone, with its attractive leaves and beautiful, pendulous flowers. It, too, can quite quickly cover pergolas, buildings and walls and looks especially good over a porch or around the front door – a suitable position for a container grown plant. Wisteria needs adequate support and must have a sunny aspect (although it is hardy up to approx $-20°F$); it flowers in May–June and although the scented mauve blooms of *Wisteria sinensis* are most typical, pink and white flowering varieties are also available.

To encourage flowering rather than foliage growth, wisterias should not be fed with a high-nitrogen fertilizer, and the same is true of climbing roses – another marvellous group of flowering climbers for containers. Useful for their flexibility and reliability, their long flowering period, good colours and sweet perfume, some of the best all-round varieties of climbing rose include 'Danse de Feu' (orange red); 'Gloire de Dijon' (pale orange double); 'Golden Showers' (golden yellow to cream); 'Guinee' (deep scarlet); 'Madame Alfred Carriere' (white) and 'Madame Gregoire Stachelin' (pink).

Finally, two slightly more unusual climbers for pots that are particular favourites of ours. *Fremontodendron californicum* 'Californian Glory' has bright golden yellow flowers which resemble huge buttercups and are produced all through the summer on fairly stiff, upright stems. It must have a south aspect and should be protected from frost. Rather more hardy (to $-20°F$) is the pretty little vine *Ampelopsis brevipedunculata* 'Elegans'. It is not rampant like some of the larger, very vigorous vines and makes an ideal plant for the side of the patio or a balcony. The leaves are its main feature, with the appealing shape and distinctive colour mix of green, silver and pink; although the plant dies back in winter, this summer effect is well worth waiting for.

Perennial plants

Perennials are of course characterized by their lush, colourful displays of spring, summer or autumn followed by a dormant winter period – and by their hardiness and reliability. In spite of their seasonal character, some – especially those with bold, distinctive leaves – make really worthwhile container plants. If they are grown as single plants in medium-sized pots (ordinary clay flower pots are fine) they can be displayed in pride of place when looking their best and then transferred to a less prominent position for over-wintering.

As in garden plant borders, most perennials in pots lend themselves well to display in informal groups rather than as single specimens and they can be very useful for a luxuriant effect in shady places. In damp shade you might group together hostas, ferns and astilbes. Hosta (sometimes known as plantain lily) is one of the best possible foliage plants for containers, forming a nicely rounded clump of leaves which fills and covers the top of the pot and in late summer is adorned by flower spikes on long stems.

There are so many varieties in existence that the American Hosta Society publishes an annual top ten chart of the most popular, and an ever increasing number are becoming known in Britain alongside the longer established and more familiar forms such as *H. fortunei* with its handsome, glaucous leaves; *H. fortunei* 'Aurea Marginata', which has more delicate green leaves edged in light yellow; *H. fortunei* 'Picta' – lighter leaves with a rich green edging – and *H. sieboldiana glauca*, which has greyish-green glaucous leaves that are very broad and ribbed.

Ferns, too, are available in abundant variety and share the usefulness of hostas for cool, shady places. Their delicate, feathery fronds make a useful break between flowering plants and the broad, bolder leaves of hostas; try grouping them in casual arrangements of three, five or seven plants together, depending on size and the space available. As for the best type to grow, some of the most charming and useful ferns have easy common names, which is just as well because their botanical names tend to be long and complicated! The male fern (*Dryopteris filix-mas*) has good long fronds that are none the less attractive for their familiarity – this is probably the best fern of all for pots. Other contenders worth considering are the hart's tongue fern (*Asplenium scolopendrium*), the lady fern (*Athyrium filix-femina*) and the ostrich feather fern (*Matteuccia struthiopteris*).

The purity and simple charm
of a white lily in a pot.

Plants

Astilbe is a plant that you will not often find recommended for container gardening, but there is no particular reason to exclude it and we feel that it makes an excellent companion for ferns and hostas in those cool, fairly shady places. Its stems are rather less sturdy and may need protection from wind, but the foliage spreads nicely near the base of the plant, filling a pot well, and the fluffy flower plumes which rise above it are enchanting. Our favourite varieties include 'Amethyst' (lilac-rose pink); 'Fanal' (deep red) and 'White Gloria', whose pure white plumes contrast well against its dark leaves.

Whilst most annual flowers require full sun, there are several flowering perennials which are well suited to container gardening and will flourish in partial shade. The day lily, *Hemerocallis*, is a real gem that is deservedly immensely popular in the United States and still becoming more prominent in Britain. Its shape is most accommodating for a pot, because the soft, spiky leaves form a dense clump which tumbles over the pot's edges forming a base against which long, slender stems throw up single, lily-shaped flowers; these may last only for a short time but are constantly replaced – a process which continues for several weeks of the summer. The bright orange, yellow and red shades make a good splash of colour against brickwork or a whitewashed wall.

Agapanthus.

Lilies en masse on the patio.

Agapanthus has a softer effect with its clustered blue flower heads, but the overall shape of the plant is similar to day lily and it would be a good alternative choice for container gardening in semi-shade. *Campanula lactiflora* has rather a different shape as a plant, but it too is excellent in pots and gives a similar impression of a soft cloud of blue with its mass of open bells on stems about 3 ft (1 m) tall.

If you are really keen on perennials in containers – and especially if you also have no plant bed space in the garden, balcony or yard – then you might like to try something a bit spectacular and grow foxgloves in 10 or 12 in (25–30 cm) diameter flowerpots (rigid plastic would be fine). Grow from plants or seed – as a biennial – and feed well during spring and early summer to encourage good growth. This should produce tall, sturdy flower spikes with a clumpy mass of leaves covering the pot. To balance the height of the flowers and conceal the bottom leaves, which are prone to untidiness, group them behind foliage plants such as hostas. A real eye-catcher.

Perennials are best grown in John Innes No. 2 compost and should be fed and watered in much the same way as shrubs, although feeding could be carried out slightly less frequently – say every two weeks. Plants should be lifted, divided and repotted when they become too large for the container; you can usually tell simply by looking that the plant has really filled tightly all the available space, but expect to re-pot roughly every two or three years. This is best carried out in early spring. In autumn, before over-wintering plants, trim dying foliage and flower stems right down to pot level.

61

Simple pot of variegated ivy
blends with planting of
geraniums and chlorophytum
at edge of paving.

Fuchsias in a decorated
Chinese pot.

Group of hostas demonstrates
the bold, lush effect of the
foliage and strong overall
shape of individual plants. The
composition is completed by
urn and pebbles.

Bulbs

Bulbs are so easy and reliable to grow that they must rate as one of the best ways of creating flower colour and effect in all kinds of containers – especially in the early months of the year, starting with the spring-flowering species crocus and little *Cyclamen coum* in January and continuing with a whole succession of snowdrops, miniature iris, narcissus, anemones, hyacinths and tulips.

Bulbs can be planted much closer together in containers than in the garden, giving a good bold display of flower; it is necessary only to ensure that they do not touch each other or the sides of the container. A more concentrated display can be achieved by planting in two or three layers, as long as bulbs are not planted directly over each other. Water well after planting and during winter months protect the container from frost.

One drawback of bulbs in plant borders is the untidy foliage after the flowers have died, but in containers this need not be a problem for once they have flowered the bulbs can be lifted from the container and heeled into an odd corner of the garden (or even a box of soil tucked out of sight if you have no plant beds) to allow their leaves to die down naturally. This leaves the containers free for immediate use with other seasonal plants such as summer bedding.

Like all container plants, bulbs require regular watering and the compost should never be allowed to dry out. If you have to leave containers for more than a week, water them thoroughly before you go and spread a mulch of damp peat over the surface of the container to conserve moisture. Bulbs need no fertilizer in containers, but they will not actually be harmed by liquid fertilizer or bone meal.

Bulbs can be grown effectively on their own in outdoor containers, and in our opinion the best impact is achieved by using one type or variety to a container, grouping them together for a pleasing mix of flowers with a colour theme of reds, yellows and cream or perhaps blue, pinks and white. Where space is very restricted – in a window box or a single container – good mixes can be planted, such as yellow narcissus with blue miniature iris or pink hyacinths with cream species crocus.

64

Really miniature bulbs can be useful where a mix of plants is required, and these are mentioned separately in connection with sink gardens. Where bulbs are used for underplanting a tree or large shrub in a container, then it is certainly desirable to stick to a single type or variety and a single colour. Planted in this way, small bulbs can be left in position to come up year after year. You could perhaps plant them a little deeper than usual to avoid disturbing them when replacing the top layer of compost or forking in any bone meal.

Bulbs that can be especially recommended for container gardening include anemone; *Chionodoxa luciliae*; crocus and colchicum (both species and hybrids); *Cyclamen coum*; galanthus; hyacinth; *Iris danfordiae* (miniature yellow); *I. reticulata* (miniature blue); muscari; *Narcissus cyclamineum*; *N. jonquilla*; *N. minnow*; *N. triandrus albus*; scilla; sternbergia and a host of tulips, including both single and double early, and species such as *T. praestans* and *T. tarda* as well as hybrids of *T. kaufmanniana*, *T. fosteriana* and *T. greigii*. All kinds of lilies and showy crown imperials are also superb.

Annuals and other seasonal flowers

For would-be container gardeners who have limited time or money – and even limited patience – annuals are a godsend. Hardly surprising that they are so popular; after all, from a few packets of seed or some plants bought at the garden centre, supermarket, greengrocer's or wherever, you can achieve fast effect and then enjoy a riot of colour for weeks and weeks. These are plants that are temporary – bright, cheerful flowers that are simple to grow, so you can have fun arranging them, experimenting to create a richly flamboyant splash, learn what works well on your patio, balcony or window box and then try something a bit different the next year.

The best effects with annuals are achieved by being extravagant. Dotted about on top of a tub they look sparse, mean and lacking in impact, but if you plant something trailing to soften the side of the pot and then as many showy flowering plants as will comfortably combine to build up a massed effect, with the centre of the tub as the highest point, you should achieve a lavish, showy display.

Once planted, the care of annuals is easy. Regular watering is obviously essential but feed sparingly or you will make all leaf growth and fewer flowers. Plants thrive best in a sunny position and you should pick off dead flowers from time to time both to encourage new growth and to keep the plant looking good.

Spring flowering seasonal plants include wallflowers, polyanthus and pansies or violas; you can use any of these alone or combined with bulb flowers.

For summer, the choice is much greater. You might go for showy geraniums (zonal pelargoniums) and gorgeous, cascading fuchsias; both types of plant are sold as standards and trailing as well as bush so you can achieve many different effects. Other useful and attractive flowers are sweet alyssum; the pot marigold (calendula); nasturtiums, which can also trail and climb; zinnia; simple, soft little candytuft; nemesia; *Phlox drummondii*; sweet scabious; lobelia for trailing and edging; brightly coloured mesembryanthemum; petunias – either self coloured or bi-colour – annual pinks and antirrinhums for a country garden look; begonias – both large, tuberous types and the little, multi-flowered *B. semperflorens* – and finally, for foliage effect, coleus; helichrysum or plants simply known as 'silver leaf', which offer quieter contrast to such a wealth of colour.

Nasturtiums have been mentioned as plants for climbing. Other annual climbers which grow fast and could be used to disguise and soften a harsh or ugly background are morning glory (ipomea); *Cobaea scandens* which has beautiful cup-shaped blue flowers; canary creeper which is a close relative of the nasturtium and bears a mass of small yellow flowers as the name suggests, and finally fragrant, old-fashioned sweet peas.

Herbs

Herbs are now so popular with cooks and gardeners alike that it is easy to buy young plants in florists and health food shops as well as more traditional places, and these are good to grow in all kinds of

Herbs in pots.

containers. You might have a trough, large bowl or box that would be suitable for a miniature herb garden or choose to grow your favourite herbs in a nicely grouped mixture of individual pots of various size and shape. Whichever method you choose, it should be possible to arrange to have them close to the house for quick, easy accessibility. This will avoid the inevitable occasion when, dressed ready for dinner guests and in need of a few sprigs of parsley, you have to run the length of a muddy garden in pouring rain in order to pick them!

Herbs grown in pots are easy to keep tidy; their aromatic leaves can scent the air on a warm summer's evening and many look pretty as well as being useful – especially the shrubby types which are in any case in regular use as garden plants. These include rosemary, thyme in numerous varieties and rue.

Most herbs need full sun, including thyme, savory, sage, rosemary, chives (which could be allowed to flower), chervil and fennel with its lovely feathery leaves. If you have a small, shady garden all is not lost for you could still grow parsley, tarragon and mint, which should be allocated its own container. Mint tends to be invasive and is inclined to overwhelm other herbs if combined in the same pot. All these three herbs require at least partial shade and all thrive in damp conditions, so keep them well watered.

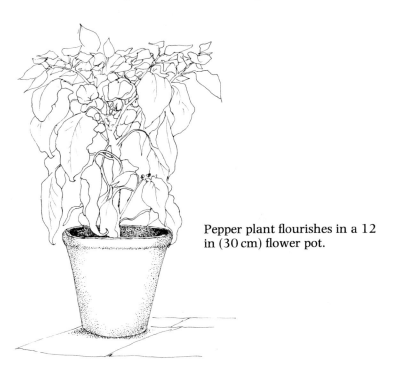

Pepper plant flourishes in a 12 in (30 cm) flower pot.

Fruit and vegetables

Even if containers are the only form of gardening available to you, it is possible to produce food from your pots. Like annuals, pot-grown vegetables are simple, quick and fun to organize. Of course, they need care, as any other container plants, but they need not be taken too seriously. Like herbs, some vegetables make rather attractive plants in their own right, particularly peppers and aubergines with ripening fruit hanging on nice bushy plants grown in a 12 in (30 cm) clay flowerpot. Plastic or natural fibre pots are equally useful and containers can be decorative or functional.

Tomatoes are familiar plants for pots and containers – especially the immensely practical growing bags that have become an almost essential part of gardening. Like peppers and aubergines, tomato plants need a sunny position. They can look good in a formal row against a wall or grouped together to create a complete produce garden in pots. Keeping plants in close proximity makes caring for them more manageable, for tomatoes should be fed frequently with an appropriate fertilizer (their requirements are different from flowers) and kept well watered, for insufficient watering leads to split and damaged fruit.

As a novelty you might grow a bush tomato in a pot – or even in a hanging basket – and you could also try runner beans in a trough against a wall, fence or shed. Fix string or canes for support and allow the plants to climb and scramble; the flowers are attractive as well as the beans and plants might be regarded as fast-growing, leafy annual climbers.

The best soft fruit for container gardening is the strawberry, which again is a rather attractive plant in its own right, especially when laden with luscious, ripening fruit. Growing plants off the ground keeps fruit clean and accessible and you could use traditional terracotta strawberry pots or the newer 'tower' pot systems which are excellent if your produce garden must be accommodated in a very limited space. A row of five tower pots burgeoning with thriving strawberry plants is just as eye-catching as a couple of pots of geraniums!

Chapter five
Sink gardens and ponds in containers

The story goes that sink gardens made their debut at the Chelsea Flower Show in 1923 and immediately captured the public imagination, creating great demand for old stone kitchen sinks and pig troughs which could be put in use as a container for a miniature rock garden. Consequently, such items which at one time had been languishing in builder's yards with a very low price tag, became both expensive and difficult to obtain. Now sink gardens seem to be enjoying a great resurgence of popularity and although the original old items may be scarce, it is possible to buy sinks and troughs manufactured for the purpose of miniature gardens – either from real stone or reconstituted stone that looks quite authentic. You might also be able to obtain an old porcelain sink which could be used in its natural state or made to look like stone with a rough-finish coating of a mix of peat, sand and cement. All sinks look better when weathered and usually only improve with time.

Position the sink in a sunny place – preferably near to the house – on firm ground such as a paved area, raising it off the ground with a low pedestal made from stone or brick piers. Alternatively it might stand on a low, wide wall. Before filling, test for drainage; if water does not run away freely it may be necessary to tilt the sink very slightly or drill an extra hole, for good drainage is essential to a successful sink garden. Cover the outlets with a layer of crocks and also spread a layer of fairly finely broken crocks on the whole floor of the sink. Over this goes a layer of pieces of rough, fibrous turf and finally the sink should be filled to within a few inches of the top with a compost specially mixed for alpines – your nursery or garden centre may be able to supply this – or you could add extra horti-

A sink garden planted with
succulents at the RHS garden,
Wisley.

cultural sand and either grit, cinterized ash pellets or finely broken crock chippings from clay flower pots to Universal compost, the lightweight version of John Innes. The main aim is to make the compost very light, gritty and free-draining.

Now comes the creative part – the artistic arrangement of rocks. Many people make the mistake of thinking that a sink garden is just a collection of alpines and dwarf conifers in fairly haphazard arrangement, but this approach misses so much of the charm of sink gardens, for they present the opportunity of creating a landscape in miniature that is artistic and well balanced yet natural-looking and avoids fussy cutesiness. A certain amount of dignity and restraint is called for, but the rocks are every bit as important as the plants.

So little rock is needed that it is worth seeking out pieces that have character and an interesting shape; you may be limited for choice as to what is available, but Westmorland, Yorkshire limestone and sandstone from Kent or Sussex can each be used to good effect. Choose a selection of pieces; for a sink garden 3 ft by 2 ft (90 cm by 60 cm) you might have them ranging in size from slightly larger than a football to about the size of a grapefruit, with some chippings and gravel for infill.

The rock should be arranged in a simple group that appears to be one single outcrop of rugged outline which has been split by frost to form deep cracks and crevices in which plants would settle. Group, say, three larger pieces towards one end of the sink and follow on from there, creating a craggy area for rock plants and a flatter one which will give the impression of an alpine meadow. It is worth spending time getting the arrangement of rocks just right, perhaps placing them, going off for lunch then returning for a second look and a readjustment.

When you feel the best possible outcrop has been created, with nice rugged lines and plenty of character from all angles, then make up the soil level around the base of the rocks and poke compost into the cracks and crevices; at this stage the whole arrangement should start to come together, and it is time to plant.

You would probably want to include one or perhaps three dwarf conifer trees, to plant on the lower slopes of the hill created from rock. One of the best is the miniature Irish juniper, *Juniperus communis* 'Compressa', and specialist growers of dwarf conifers list many other suitable varieties of *Chamaecyparis, Pinus, Juniperus, Taxus, Picea* and so on. When dwarf trees and shrubs are decided upon, you can choose from the very wide range of rock and alpine plants available. Most of them cost little and many have delightful, delicate foliage and a mass of tiny, brilliantly coloured flowers. Those that thrive naturally in rock crevices will obviously be appropriate for planting in nooks and crannies in the pieces of rock whilst miniature meadow plants and low-growing alpines should be planted in the flatter areas around the rock 'outcrop'.

Recommended plants for the rocks include encrusted or aizoon forms of *Saxifraga*, especially *S. aizoon baldensis*, which has tiny greyish green rosettes of leaves, and also any of the 'Kabschia' types of saxifrage. *Armeria caespitosa* – a miniature thrift – is good for a sunny crevice and all sorts of dwarf campanulas are lovely; another familiar flower is the rock garden pink and the dwarf mountain forget-me-not, *Myosotis rupicola* is a must. Finally, there are many suitable varieties of rock primulas and for a dense cushion of foliage which will hang over the edge of the sink *Silene acaulis* is valuable.

For the 'alpine meadow' area you might choose from *Allium cyaneum*, a dainty Chinese garlic; *Antennaria dioica* 'Minima'; alpine gentian; the smallest and most compact mossy phloxes such as *Phlox douglasii* 'Red Admiral', *P. douglasii rosea* and *P. douglasii* 'Waterloo'; *Raoulia australis*, which forms mats of silvery grey foliage and *Sisyrinchium brachypus* which bears yellow flowers above tufty blades of foliage. Other excellent choices can be made from small bulb flowers including various crocuses, grape hyacinth; miniature iris and the really miniature narcissi such as the charming little 'Tete-a-Tete'.

As an alternative to this now traditional approach to the sink garden, you could devote the planting entirely to a selection of various types of *Sempervivum* or houseleek or you might choose to make a miniature forest landscape using different dwarf trees with only very low, creeping plants to form a carpet beneath – thyme and *Raoulia* would be suitable. Yet another more unusual choice might

73

Not a pond in a container, but containers beside a pond. This modern town garden was designed in the style of Gertrude Jekyll by students of Merrist Wood college. The gold colour theme features bright yellow daisy chrysanthemums in handsome urns.

be a miniature garden in Japanese style, with dwarf shrubs like rhododendrons as well as conifers; here the rock formations would play an important role, for the aim should be to recreate the restrained understatement of the Japanese style rather than a confection of little bridges and lanterns.

A pond in a container

Water brings an added dimension to any garden – a reflective surface that is fascinating when rippling with movement and soothing when still. If you have a tiny concrete yard or want to take water to a part of the garden where there is no space for a full-scale pond, then there is no need to miss out. As long as you can find a sunny spot, it is possible to make a pond in a container, whether this is wide and shallow or a dramatic and more bulbous decorated Chinese earthenware egg pot.

Obviously the pot should have no holes in the bottom and will additionally need to be waterproofed. This can be done by painting on the inside surface a sealing layer of waterproof pond paint. Available from garden centres and water garden specialists, the paint usually comes in a buff stone or bluish turquoise shade and its application should be carried out in warm, dry weather to allow it to dry properly and seal the pot effectively.

A mixture of loam and shingle in the bottom of the container pond will enable you to plant aquatic subjects, or you could grow a single miniature water lily in an aquatic basket and drop one or two floating plants on to the water surface. The dwarf water lily, *Nymphaea pygmaea*, and other named varieties will grow in up to about a 6 in (15 cm) depth of water, in full sun, and will offer the full beauty of the familiar flowers. It is wise to buy a dwarf lily from a water specialist to ensure that you obtain the right plant, as there is sometimes confusion surrounding dwarf varieties.

There are some fascinating floating plants that you might try, including water moss; water hyacinth; water lettuce (tender so regard it as an annual addition) and water soldier. Neither are plants the only possibility for an intriguing, floating addition to the pond surface. We like to float hollow plastic pebbles which glide gently across the water, bumping and bobbing, or the green glass floats from old fishing nets that you see in seaside gift shops. The effect on a sunny day with a gentle breeze blowing can be quite mesmerizing and is perhaps a good alternative to that fascinating pastime of watching fish darting and swimming, for a pond in a container is not really big enough to support a fish on a permanent basis.

It is nice to position your container pond close to where you sit outside or in a place where it can be seen from indoors. It would also make a compelling feature beside the front door – perhaps on an enlarged, paved step area. If the pond is accessible to the house, you could make an even more interesting feature by adding a fountain. Position the smallest type of submersible circulating pump in the base of the pool, concealing it and the cable with pebbles and plants as far as possible. The cable runs to a transformer which converts the power supply from an ordinary indoor socket to a very low voltage for economy and – most importantly – safety.

All this is for long-term effect, but if you are having a summer party or barbecue you could make an instant pond in almost any kind of watertight bowl or trough – perhaps a nice earthenware pot from indoors. A magical effect can be achieved simply by floating on the water surface lighted candles (the dumpy, night-light variety) and three or five open blooms of a perfumed rose.

Hydrangea in reproduction
Tudor jardiniere.

Chapter six
Planting containers for visual effect

In introducing the range of plants that are suited to container gardening, we mentioned the importance of composing plant or plants and pot as a complete ornamental feature in its own right, creating an overall effect that is well shaped and balanced. This approach to the whole process of planting containers so that they look right – whether the desired effect is soft and pretty or strikingly dramatic – cannot be overemphasized. Container gardening is, after all, a visual art and no artistic object is pleasing to look at if the shape is unbalanced, giving an uncomfortable impression of being top or bottom heavy or awkwardly lumpy rather than with graceful flowing lines. Even if a dramatic, abstract impression is intended, the composition should still balance or have some distinct, discernible purpose to its form. As for detail, simplicity so often works best; an over-complicated mass of different shapes and colours becomes jumbled and confusing; one soon tires of its busyness.

So it is with plants. In borders, successful plant combinations are the challenge because the overall effect depends on a host of different plants which, whilst offering variation of height, shape, colour and form, nevertheless harmonize to paint a complete picture. Container gardening is, on the other hand, perhaps closer to the art of painting individual masterpieces – single cameos which are almost deceptive in their simplicity because every time you look at them you seem to see something new, to appreciate afresh their shape or some particular detail.

How can these artistic principles be applied to the practicalities of planting containers? To return first to the most practical aspect of all, the pot, trough, urn, tub or whatever must be sufficiently large and sufficiently substantial to support the plant for which it is going to provide a home. We have already made several specific suggestions when describing both the range of pots available and the range of plants recommended for container gardening, but our own experience leads us to the conclusion that it is almost impossible to lay down hard and fast guidelines, especially if appearance is just as important as horticultural requirements. However, since the charm rating of a dead plant is absolutely nil, it may help to pass on the basic principles of our own approach to container gardening which attempts to maintain a constantly changing and growing collection of plants that are healthy and thriving yet make pleasing visual compositions.

Firstly, we stick to the general principle of a single variety of plant to each container, especially for trees, shrubs, conifers and perennials, with the possible exception of a few small bulbs planted informally beneath a deciduous weeping tree. We keep a stock of containers of various types (mostly terracotta – both plain and decorated – and glazed earthenware because they happen to appeal to our taste) and, perhaps more importantly for our purpose here, various sizes ranging from 6 in (15 cm) diameter through 9, 12, 15, 18, 20 and 24 in (23, 30, 38, 45, 50 and 60 cm) and some even larger.

A new plant is allocated the largest container in which it is possible to achieve a balanced look; for trees and tall conifers this is likely to be 24 (60 cm) or even 30 in (75 cm) diameter and 18 to 24 in (45 to 60 cm) deep. If it is evident that for a while the composition is obviously going to look pot-heavy, then the tree or shrub might be positioned slightly off-centre and a balanced impression introduced by spreading a layer of stone chippings over the soil surface, with a piece of rock or a group of pebbles.

A shrub – and certainly perennials – may be planted in the size of container that looks right – or perhaps just slightly too large – for its present proportions, in the knowledge that after a while we will have to upgrade, repotting it into a larger container. Obviously, all our container plants are assiduously watered and fed, using either general purpose liquid fertilizer or a mix made up from one of

Chempak's range of granular compounds for more specific groups of plants. However, as soon as a tree or shrub begins to look sickly – perhaps the leaves are yellowing or are shed too early – then it is repotted into a larger container, and if this is impossible then it is planted in the garden and replaced. Perennials, which in our case mainly consist of a large collection of hostas, are lifted from their pots and split as necessary in the way already mentioned in the section on perennial plants.

This continuing process illustrates the fact that once you start to take an interest in container gardening, you build up knowledge and experience and in time become confident of making judgements based on that experience, assessing the needs of plants and becoming tuned to their requirements. You also learn over a period of time which plants look best and thrive in certain positions in what is now fashionably known as the microclimate of your own garden, for each site is different not only in terms of wind and shelter, sun and shade but also in its visual requirements. Where is the best place for that beautiful acer so that it can be seen from the dining table or the kitchen sink?

To return once again to the subject of visual composition, our approach to combining container and plant is to arrange the plant so that it is shown off to its best advantage and yet looks natural, echoing its natural inclination and growth habit. It is almost impossible to adhere to this principle with bold shrubs on the basis of more than one type to a container, for there is simply not enough space.

Balance of shape and proportion between plant and pot.

Three different views of a
courtyard garden where
paving and wall are softened
by a combination of plant beds
and planted pots used both
individually and in groups.
Pots as well as plants are
chosen for shape, colour and
style to blend with hand-made
bricks, natural sawn York
paving and blue garden
furniture. (Garden designed by
Faith and Geoff Whiten for
Halifax Building Society.)

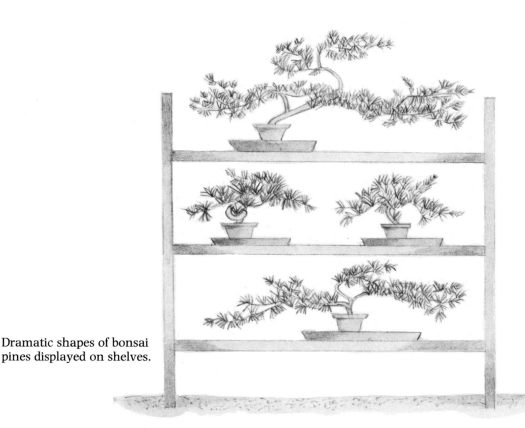

Dramatic shapes of bonsai
pines displayed on shelves.

Almost inevitably, the plants merge together as they grow and the
shape and form of each individual specimen is lost in an amorphous
mass. However, it is possible to achieve a good, natural effect using,
say, one bold, upright shrub with a ground-hugging plant such as
thyme set to one side or with rock or pebbles, as described. The
miniature landscape concept of a sink garden is also an important
exception because the approach is quite different, although the aim
is still to display tiny individual plants to their best advantage.

Temporary flowering plants do lend themselves to slightly more
flamboyant treatment, but whether you choose to combine two
different types in one container or to display a bold splash of a single
type and colour, the principle of arrangement for good shape and
effect yet a fairly natural, comfortable look should still apply. This
skill is akin to the arrangement of cut flowers in what might be
termed the natural rather than the tortured school! Of course some
people may prefer a contrived and more formal, regimented look

84

rather along the lines of formal bedding displays, and this must be a matter of personal taste and opinion. However, to us that style tends to represent the heavy hand of man insisting on controlling and regimenting nature, rather than a lightness of touch which merely helps nature to tell its own story.

To arrange a mass of geraniums, petunias, pansies, polyanthus or fuchsias in a pot, fill it with compost to within a few inches of the top – just enough to support the plants so that their stems lean outwards at a gentle angle to the rim of the pot. Arrange plants around the edge of the pot leaning them in this way so that they are at slightly different levels – not too regular – and then, depending on the size of the plants and of the pot, either make a second circle of plants towards the centre, placing these in a more upright position but with a slight outward lean and finish with one plant as an upright centrepiece, or simply fill in with one central plant. As you go, try to arrange the plants so that their leaves and flowers merge without any large gaps. Finally fill in carefully around the base of the stems with compost, drawing back the leaves to avoid making them too dirty; firm the plants well into position and water well, sprinkling the leaves and flowers to clean off any remaining compost.

Seasonal flowers like these will look much better in a bold, well-shaped display. The beauty of the flowers is lost if plants are just clumped together in an upright position and the whole composition may look pot-heavy. The blooms are quite delicate and it is worth making some effort to avoid the sad imbalance of a few little flowers looking lost and flat on top of a heavy, imposing container. Similarly, it can be effective to counter-balance a standard geranium, fuchsia or daisy-like *Chrysanthemum frutescens* by planting around the base of the stem some small variegated trailing ivy, bought as indoor pot plants.

Pink hydrangea with blue and white campanulas. Each pot is planted to create a rounded mass of flowers and the three together make a balanced group.

Astelia 'Silver Spear' is a New Zealand plant that is ideal for a sheltered patio. Its distinctive colouring and shape (similar to phormium) are dramatic as an individual specimen.

Pink pebbles echo the colour of
pinks and fuchsias, making a
real feature of a corner
surfaced simply in gravel.

Chapter seven
Where and how to use plants in containers

If you take care – in the way that we have already advised – to match and combine plant and container so that they make a pleasing, balanced composition, then it would be a great shame to allow your creation to hide its light under a bushel by tucking it away in a corner or, conversely, to make it centre of attention in the wrong way so that Granny trips over the base as soon as she sets foot outside the patio door! Containers can add interest and high points to a garden, introducing plants to soften and decorate paved areas and even hiding or disguising less desirable features that cannot be removed.

When you really think about it, listing the ways in which you can use container plants seems almost endless – rather like a parlour game – and in this chapter we set out to give just some ideas that have worked for us in situations we have known. Although we are talking about the garden and house in general terms, some ideas would lend themselves equally to small spaces – a backyard, a tiny space between house frontage and pavement, a balcony or a roof garden.

We have mentioned before the fact that an apparently random grouping of plants in pots looks best and most natural if it is quite carefully composed, whilst avoiding an overdone, contrived look. As with plants in a border or bed, a group of pots is most effective in an odd number – three, five seven or even more – as this makes possible a slightly asymmetrical arrangement with a pleasantly irregular outline. At its simplest, you might make a group of three using one large and two smaller containers in the same or complementing shape and material.

A larger group in an open position will be seen from several directions, so it is best to place the tallest and boldest plants close to the centre, graduating down to quite low or delicate plants in interesting containers around the edge of the group. These should form a slightly irregular line. Against a background, you would obviously place taller plants at the back and shorter ones in front, but avoiding a boring shape by occasionally bringing a taller shape forward. Individual tall plants in containers can be balanced by two lower, bushy plants placed slightly to one side. Various colour effects can be achieved, but the accepted principles of floristry could be applied if you are uncertain – use brighter, bolder colours at the back or centre of the arrangement and softer, paler colours to the front.

Containers on the patio

No patio or paved area in the garden would be complete without planted containers; they do so much to enliven the area, adding height and natural colour which should ideally complement the shade and texture of the paving. A good practical use for a patio planter is to disguise a drain inspection cover. Access should never be blocked, but a container can readily removed to one side as the occasion arises; you might choose either a box on castors or a group of three small pots that do not weigh too heavily.

Pots disguising a drain inspection cover.

Containers should obviously be placed away from main pedestrian routes; to one side of the area you could position a single stunning plant in a pot or a group as large as space permits. Climbing plants in pots can also be placed at the base of timber pergola supports where this shelters a seating area; it will be greatly enhanced and softened, creating a really pleasant and secluded feeling.

Many of our garden designs include a patio set at an angle of 45° to the back of the house, and this creates a corner jutting into the garden – often a leading-off point for a path through the lawn. Just to one side of this corner is a good place for a pot. Also, should the patio include a change in level, containers could be used as markers to indicate the low step and guide people towards the path that you actually wish them to take.

With architectural features

A building or structural feature can be made to look more imposing and self-important by formal plants such as pyramid bays or tall conifers in pots especially if they are placed on either side of the entrance. In contrast, informal tubs with softly trailing plants can soften a front door, making it look more friendly and welcoming. Just one tub containing a wisteria or climbing rose that scrambles over the porch has much the same effect.

Steps present excellent opportunities to have fun with pots and plants. If they are sufficiently wide, place one at either side of each step, using identical containers and plants such as tulips, daffodils, geraniums, box or dwarf conifers for a formal look. The scene will change gear instantly if you then add smaller pots of ivy, single fuchsias, trailing lobelia or silver helichrysum, interlacing them around the original sentinels. If you really want to clothe the sides of the steps or a wall beside them, grow climbers like the annual canary creeper or shrubby *Clematis montana*. Obviously you should always allow sufficient space for the steps to be negotiated in safety.

With walls

For a really classical look that is almost tongue-in-cheek you might indulge in the ultimate in wall pots – a classical urn with ringed

Tubs of tulips line steps in
formal manner.

handles set on top of each pier in a long brick wall. More modest effects can be achieved just to the end of a wall – either on top or around the base or both. On a high wall you might position a climbing plant in a pot, allowing it to grow downwards.

Corners where two walls meet can be harsh in line and make rather stark, even boring places. These are ideal spots for a group of container plants; in a shady corner it might be lilies and crown imperials to the rear with hostas and ferns in front and in a sunny position you could place one magnificent tub of hydrangea or a mature yucca. Alternatively you could go for a group of three phormiums – one large *P. tenax* with two plants of the variegated 'Yellow Wave' in front. Flowering groups in the sun could include a pink rose with pots of white petunias and cerise and white fuchsias. The possibilities are endless.

Again, climbers in pots are invaluable against a wall, fence or trellis whether they are permanent plants or more seasonal sweet peas, trailing nasturtium, convolvulus or canary creeper.

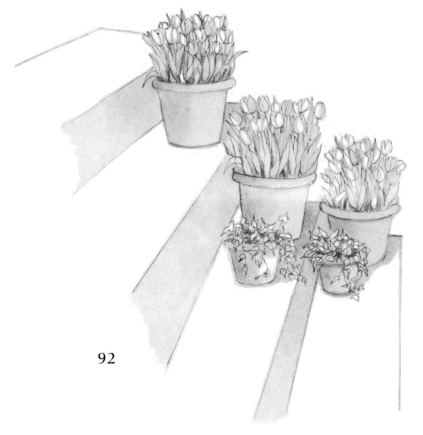

More tulips and little pots of ivy make for a more informal look.

92

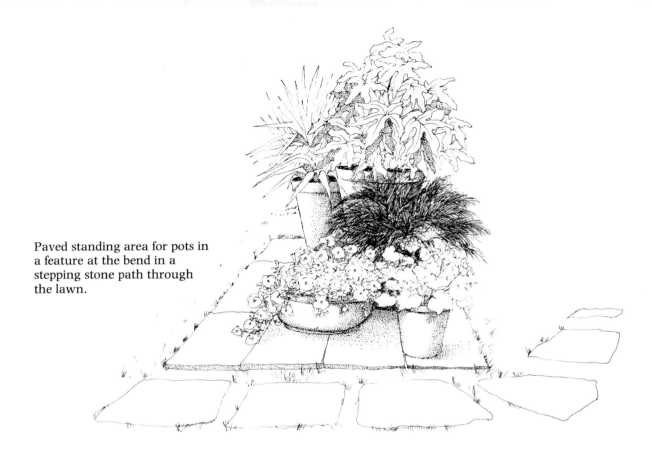

Paved standing area for pots in a feature at the bend in a stepping stone path through the lawn.

In the garden generally

If you create a 'dry' garden consisting of paving slabs, set at intervals in shingle or stone chippings, decorated with pebbles and softened by low, creeping ground cover plants, then planted containers are an essential addition to complete the picture, whether a single stunning conifer with an unusual shape, introducing a hint of the oriental, or a tub of fuchsias bringing colour and a more luxuriant look.

Pots do not have to be sited in an open position – they can often make a somewhat surprising punctuation in a plant bed or border, whether planted or unplanted. You can enjoy creating a sense of mystery, with the pot half-hidden, of surprise as you come across it on rounding a corner or of imposing grace and beauty as a decorated urn stands out against a background of dark green foliage.

The junctions of paths make natural positions for containers – at the corner of the lawn or where the path to the front door joins the drive. Too sharp an angle at this point often creates the maddening

93

Group of pots softening the
corner of a wall includes
variegated *Pseudopanax* 'Gold
Splash' – a lush patio plant
that needs winter protection.

Single Christmas tree adds
distinction to the house
frontage. The squared lawn
has been cut away in a
sweeping curve and the pot
stands on gravel to avoid a
corner trodden down by foot
traffic.

95

situation of a worn corner of grass regularly downtrodden by the short-cut path taken by the postman, the milkman and everyone's children (plus bikes). Put a stop to this by cutting back the edge of the lawn to form a curve; fill in the corner between this and the path/drive junction with shingle, and position on it a specimen shrub or tree in a large, heavy pot. They will be forced to take the path.

A path which leads through a lawn the length of the garden can be boring if uninterrupted. When it takes a turn or reaches a natural staging point, it can be made much more interesting by a punctuation in the form of a small, square area of paving or a grid of stepping stones designed as a base for the display of planted pots.

A purpose-built display

This takes us back to the 'how' rather than the 'where' of showing off plants in containers. Rather than look around the garden and then find container plants for those awkward or dreary corners, you might want to create a setting which allows for the impressive display of treasured plants that you already possess.

An architectural plant deserves to be displayed against a backdrop that shows up its structure, shape and outline. A screen can do this admirably; it might be made from proofed canvas fabric – either plain or with an eye-catching design – stretched on a timber frame; from vertical bamboo poles with horizontal ties in oriental style or from painted or stained timber.

Plants can also be displayed closer to eye level, arranged on and beside an old bench or table or on an open set of shelves rather like an outdoor form of room divider. This would be a good means of displaying small bulbs or alpines grown in shallow pans or bonsai plants. You might, alternatively, make a more structural and immovable feature like a raised, square plinth that is paved over, as a surface for the display of plants in pots arranged with pebbles or other incidental decoration. Similarly a raised timber deck of the same proportions makes a sunny place for lounging and alongside a rug, cushions and a tray of drinks what would look better than a little wooden tub spilling over with flowers?

96

Bamboo is highlighted
by a screen with oriental
decoration.

As a garden feature

En masse, pots, troughs, tubs and urns are capable of being formal
as well as informal – of doing a job as well as looking pretty. A
straight row of identically planted containers make an excellent
hedge, edging or demarcation and is somehow fascinating in its
symmetry and regularity. Quite a different kind of feature can be
created by using containers in composition with other ornamental
objects – perhaps a piece of sculpture, a single chair with a beautiful
shape (whether discarded or in use) or with one of our favourite
simple decorative devices – a group of pebbles. Carefully arranged
yet entirely random in appearance, such a group can introduce
relief of shape and texture as well as being employed to balance
shapes and sizes of pots. A pot on its own looks good, but that same
pot with a little group of pebbles set to one side somehow becomes a
complete decorative feature which makes its own statement.

97

Planted pots used as an important part of a complete garden feature. The Buddha and stones create a restful, timeless mood and the individual plants – including conifers, acer and echeverias grown in their own pot with stone chippings – each has a strong sculptural quality.

As sculpture

Some plants in pots hardly need to be associated with other ornamental objects, for they have taken on the role of a piece of sculpture in their own right – those plants with bold architectural shape like cordyline, *Fatsia japonica* or yucca. As such, they work well as a centrepiece – perhaps the focal point of an area paved in a design of concentric circles, or in pride of place in an open area, set on top of an imposing pedestal.

In fact they can, of course, fulfil the role that an actual piece of sculpture would fill and so lend themselves to any position where a statue or ornament would be appropriate. Perhaps most dramatic might be at the end of a long vista and the most intimate in the shelter of a wall niche.

With water

A pond needs an open, sunny situation and yet this often means that it is located some distance from plant borders, in which case it can tend to look rather bare and isolated. The obvious solution is to soften with plants and one of the most convenient ways of doing this is to position plants in containers in close proximity. With an informal pond, keep it fairly simple and as natural as possible; perennials like hemerocallis, agapanthus or astilbe in a pot would be appropriate as would a weeping Kilmarnock willow tree, a corkscrew hazel or a simple tub of geraniums.

Formal ponds that are square, rectangular or circular in shape – and if not actually set in paving will probably have paved surround – offer even more flexibility and you might display an *Acer palmatum*, a *Cedrus deodara* or other weeping conifer, a tub of fuchsias; almost any small weeping tree or a group selected from these. Ivy would also be good, as would bamboo, and the soft petals of white petunias echo the water's surface as they seem to flutter and ripple in a breeze.

The surround of a swimming pool can look rather bare and spartan and plants in containers can create a softer, more welcoming feel. In this setting the scale demands something really bold and possibly slightly exotic. You could certainly get away with the

Mediterranean feel of a yucca or cordyline and a formal row of box or bay trees in white painted tubs would be quite stunning, as would standard geranums, fuchsias, roses or *Chrysanthemum frutescens* Bold blue hydrangeas in a stone tub would mix well with smaller pots of almost any white flowers, echoing the blue of the pool.

In the spotlight

The display of container plants need not be limited to daylight hours, for with simple lighting effects even a single plant – especially one with fine, delicate foliage or a bold, sculptural shape – can take on a magical look. Probably the simplest and safest system of garden lighting consists of a series of lamps which can be fixed simply by clipping to any point on a waterproof cable. They run on a similar principle to a low-voltage fountain pump; you plug into an ordinary indoor socket (or wire into a wall switch if you are competent with electrics) and the current is converted to a very low voltage by a transformer.

As for lighting effects, it is a good idea to experiment a little, using different coloured filters (blue or green enhance foliage plants beautifully) and positioning the lamps in different places. Shining towards the plant as a spotlight or floodlight shows off the detail of the leaves against a dark background. A more unusual and dramatic effect occurs if the plant is illuminated from behind, at ground level – glowing leaves which look quite different from the familiar daylight impression.

Chapter eight
Balconies and roof gardens

A balcony may offer very limited space, but it presents a great deal of scope for container gardening; you could create a tiny garden in Japanese style with a specimen conifer and rhododendrons or camellias and finish with pebbles and a buddha or stone lantern; a formal, classical look with shrubs in white painted Versailles tubs and a white painted chair to match or simply a cheerful, riotous mass of colour. Whatever your taste, do ensure that the balcony is sufficiently strong to support the weight of your miniature garden; another point that may be relevant is that some apartment blocks have restrictions written into the terms of the lease, preventing residents from allowing plants to trail ostentatiously over the outside of the balcony – especially where the building has particular historic or architectural interest.

Although balcony plants may be seen from the road or the building on the opposite side of the street, your main concern is what you will see from your living room or bedroom and so it is a good idea to choose a colour scheme that will match the interior decor, adding a touch of class and showing that you have really thought the scheme through, giving it a designer finish.

On a sunny balcony the scope is greatest. If you have any combination which includes red, orange, yellow, brown or green for the interior decor, you might have pots and troughs planted with red geraniums, pot marigolds, white geraniums and coleus with leaves coloured fresh green, yellow and brown. For the house wall or the balcony wall or railings you could train yellow flowering canary creeper or trailing nasturtium and plant wall pots with red and orange busy lizzies. Another good finishing touch would be golden

Climbers of all sorts are useful
for balconies and roof gardens.
This rose has been trained on
a traditional bower.

Balcony garden with Japanese feel.

variegated ivy like *Hedera helix* 'Buttercup'. Scented flowers are gorgeous for a summer evening; try nicotiana and golden thyme and sage in pots.

In spring this balcony could look equally good if pots, troughs, boxes and pans are filled with yellow and orange narcissus; *Tulipa praestans* 'Fusilier' which has a multi-flowering head of rich scarlet; yellow crocus; *Iris danfordiae* (a miniature yellow iris); cream hyacinths and cream Dutch tulips. For a touch of drama, add a few pots of orange and yellow crown imperials.

Where the indoor colour scheme includes blues, pinks and lavender your summer planting might be based on deep pink fuchsias; soft pink petunias; white geranium; sweet alyssum; blue lobelia and ageratum with annual silver leaf; chlorophytum and white or silver variegated ivy with a tiny leaf that looks almost painted. As climbers, try blue morning glory and multi-coloured sweet peas or the lovely little pink, silver and green variegated vine *Ampelopsis brevipedunculata* 'Elegans', which could remain as a permanent plant. The sweet peas should be scented but you might also grow silver-

104

leaf thyme, *Thymus* 'Silver Queen'. The overall effect would be one of soft, delicate charm and prettiness.

Bulbs for pink, blue and white spring colour include snowdrops, scilla, muscari, miniature *Iris reticulata*, soft pink and white hyacinths and the lovely pink and white water lily tulip *Tulipa kaufmanniana* 'Heart's Delight'. In autumn tiny cyclamen add a delicate hint of mauve and pink.

If the balcony is north facing, your choice of plants is obviously more limited but you could still achieve a lush, soft effect for many months by growing in pots ferns, hostas, astilbes, ivies, *Fatsia japonica* and camellias as well as the small flowered *Clematis montana*, either pink or white. This is a mass of bloom in May, but it can be rather rampant so you may need to keep the growth trimmed.

Containers for roof gardens

Much of the general approach that we have described for balconies can also be applied to roof gardens, but a roof garden does have an extra quality of its own – that sense of intrigue and delight at sitting above the rooftops in a private, secluded garden – possibly with the added attraction of stunning views. The roof garden with which we are most familiar really consists only of a paved area and parapet walls, but being situated in London's docklands, it offers on one side a panorama of the River Thames with its mixture of tower blocks, tiny old pubs, warehouses, cranes and the occasional passing tourist boat or police launch and on the other the assembled ranks of city offices, which appear to be stacked and slotted on top of each other, the unmistakable round dome of St Paul's Cathedral in their midst. Each view is equally compelling and one can spend quite a long time contemplating both broad scope and detail.

To return to basic practicalities, there is not scope here to describe in detail the structural requirements and considerations of roof gardens, but it must be said that you should check the structure with a surveyor or building inspector before you do anything, ensuring not only that the building will take the weight but that there is adequate provision for drainage of surplus water. The next vital point is safety

Hydrangea in front of an ornamental timber screen, which would help provide the shelter vital to roof gardens.

Azalea in a Chinese display of container plants. Purpose-built shelves and walls can be useful for showing smaller plants to their best advantage.

Tall ivies (expertly trained on canes by Geest Horticulture) in the corner of a sheltering wall. Variation in height is achieved by standing one on another upturned container.

Cheerful annuals – good for
balcony or roof garden.

and a roof garden should obviously be enclosed by sturdy walls or
fences to a height which may be stipulated by the local authority. In
any case, a fairly high screen of some description can be an advantage both to your own comfort and the well-being of plants, for
the main problem on a roof is wind, which can dry out pots very
quickly and damage leaves and flowers.

When planning containers for a roof garden, make full use of both
floor and wall space but do remember that everything you use will
have to be lugged up stairs or in a lift and along hallways – and that
includes pots, compost and plants! It is sensible to plan an overall
layout as you would any garden design, perhaps making raised
boxes which would be supplemented by individual pots and troughs
in a lightweight material if necessary.

108

Perhaps most successful is a range of plants for a year-round interest, introducing all the elements you would expect to find in a garden at ground level. Climbers would be particularly important, but you could also include at least one weeping tree and two or three conifers – pine might be a good choice as the foliage is less susceptible to wind damage and plants are generally pretty hardy. A few specimen shrubs would also be appropriate and perennials and annuals would add seasonal colour. Our old friends the spring flowering bulbs would once again be reliable and hardy for a splash of colour.

Finally, on both balconies and roof gardens container plants will be greatly enhanced if they are combined with sculpture, pebbles or other ornaments and if you experiment with lighting effects.

Chapter nine
Window boxes and wall pots

Clean windows, glossy paintwork, pretty curtains and well-maintained brickwork all help to make the façade of a house look neat, tidy and welcoming but the addition of a single well-planted window box really brings the scene to life. It is almost like a means of communication between the occupant and passers-by.

Among the most popular and effective window boxes are those made in wood, whether it is treated to give a neutral finish or painted a colour to blend with the finish of the house and the shade of the paintwork. Some striking effects are possible – red flowers in a black or very dark brown box on a red-brick house or red and white flowers in a navy blue box on a whitewashed cottage with blue paintwork. Curtains, too, are a good starting point for a colour scheme and when the box needs repainting you could go for a completely new look. On a small scale, there is scope to use window box plants to create distinctive colour effects like those described for container planting on balconies.

Before considering ways of planting window boxes, it is important to make a vital practical point regarding fixing, for boxes *must* be supported and fixed securely to avoid accidents, especially if they are situated some distance off the ground and could cause a nasty accident if they were to fall. In any case, the weight of box, soil and plants combined would be so great that the minimum disaster would be a broken box, shattered plants and compost all over the place.

As for the style of window box planting, there are two main approaches. You could go for a fairly formal, classical look and use a single type of plant en masse – or perhaps a mixture of two. A good

Effective simplicity. Flowers
complement stone in this
window box outside the Pump
Room at Bath.

choice might be hyacinths, narcissus or polyanthus in spring and petunias, busy lizzies or geraniums for summer. The effect will be both bold and simple and well suited to an urban setting or a building in classical architectural style. The neat lines and colour of the box combined with a bushy splash of flower colour make a sophisticated combination. In this setting, it is important to keep flowers looking tidy and to remove dead heads as often as necessary.

For a cottage or any more rural setting, you might find it more appropriate to go for flamboyant, luxuriant informality. As with formal window boxes, plan for two rows of plants to give maximum impact, but to the front of the box plant climbers which will either trail downwards or climb up around the window and in the centre and rear of the box position lower, bushier plants.

For a permanent trailer or climber you could choose ivy, but for summer effect any of the annual climbers would work admirably, growing quickly to hug the sides of the window in a charmingly wayward manner. As trailers, they will soon form a dramatic mass of tumbling flowers and foliage.

In winter, window boxes can look sad and neglected and it is a good idea to plant dwarf conifers and heathers or a bushy evergreen like thyme. Again, ivy really comes into its own in winter; there are so many varieties of *Hedera helix* from which to choose that you could create a mixture of green gold, pale yellow, white and silver using ivies alone. Any gaps can always be filled with a little group of three lightweight plastic pebbles set into the soil and partially covered with foliage.

112

Dwarf tomatoes and runner beans newly planted...

...and a few weeks later –
food from your window box!

If you want to change the contents of a window box for a constant succession of seasonal flower, you could simply use the box as a container into whch you position plants bought from the garden centre ready growing in pots. Arrange them in the box and then pack damp peat around the pots; this will keep them in place and help to conserve moisture, which will be lost more quickly than if the plants were growing in a box full of compost. This method of window box gardening is ideal for those who live in a city apartment and have no suitable place in which to plant up boxes in the usual way. It is also extremely quick and easy; when plants are past their best the pots can be lifted out carefully and diposed of with the household rubbish.

If you have even a tiny space outdoors in which to keep a few boxes, you could adopt the 'shell' box principle, planting up plastic or fibre troughs which slide in and out of the wooden window box as a complete, ready growing unit. With bulbs, for example, you could plant two boxes in autumn – one with early bulbs like crocus and snowdrops combined with polyanthus or pansies and the other with

113

Spring window box features
iris, narcissus and trailing ivy.

later flowering bulbs like tulips, either alone or in a suitable combination.

In this way, you can protect planted boxes over winter and have them ready for an organized succession of flowering. They can also be used not just once but from year to year. Leave the bulbs in the boxes after flowering and water them for several weeks with diluted liquid fertilizer; they should remain quite happily in the boxes without lifting and with no need to replace the compost.

Wall pots

Troughs which can be attached to a wall with brackets have a similar use to window boxes, but their position can be more flexible, introducing flowers and foliage to a bare expanse of brickwork. However, they really look well only if used at no more than waist height and it is not difficult to arrange plants in free-standing containers to do a similar job.

Much more useful are wall pots. Whether you hang them on a wall or fence or build shelves into a new wall upon which pots can simply be stood, this is an excellent way of introducing plants above eye level. In a new garden walls and fences desperately need softening, but climbers take time to mature. A group of wall pots not only brings instant life and colour high up on the structure, it also gives the added artistic opportunity of creating a pleasing pattern in the arrangement of the pots, whether formally symmetrical or informally random – a wandering group of five or seven.

Wall pots are becoming more popular and an ever increasing range of designs is available. You might choose a terracotta pot with bulbous, rounded front and flat back which hangs on a single hook and would look good containing just white lobelia or a couple of

busy lizzies. Wall baskets virtually take the form of half a hanging basket and are fitted flush to the structure which they are to decorate. Their open framework allows you to poke in trailing plants at frequent intervals, creating a mass of cascading growth that obscures the basket after a very short time.

Whether you choose, pots or baskets, the end result should be the same – a cheerful exuberance of plants that add a vital touch of softness and fresh, living interest to the buildings in which we spend our time, whether for work or leisure, in public bustle or quiet privacy.

Chapter ten
Hanging baskets

Whilst freestanding pots and tubs decorate the garden at ground level, hanging baskets introduce a new dimension to container gardening with charm, interest and a softening quality at eye level and above. In the garden itself they can be suspended from the cross-beam of a pergola (check for strength of support before fixing) or you might even build a simple system of uprights and cross beams in an L shape. This is a particularly useful device in a new garden or one where there are few mature trees and plants because it creates an instant opportunity for plant interest above eye level when everything around seems rather flat. In this setting, a series of baskets set at different levels in irregular, random pattern would be an eye-catching feature right through the summer, and possibly in winter months too if you choose some of the year-round plants recommended towards the end of this chapter.

Suspended from a wall bracket, hanging baskets can decorate a porch or house wall, a balcony or verandah and even a garage or rather unattractive outbuilding. We once inherited a concrete storage shed which was too useful to remove but desperately ugly to look at; hanging baskets wrought the perfect transformation. Again, safety is important – do ensure that brackets are securely fixed and avoid placing baskets where people may hit their head or where the drips from watering will damage anything underneath.

Various types of hanging basket are available, from simple wire mesh (often plastic covered) to a solid plastic pot with saucer or a hanging clay pot. Ideally, the aim should be to hide the basket entirely with boldly cascading plants, so the appearance of the basket need not be too important. However, if you choose to go for a more

118

Hanging basket with fuchsias.

delicate look and make the pot or basket a feature in itself then a more decorative style would obviously be important.

A wire mesh basket should be lined with a thick layer of sphagnum moss which has previously been well moistened; you could even moisten it in a weak solution of liquid fertilizer to give plants an extra start. A more modern alternative for lining is a purpose made basket liner in a fibrous, felt-like material. Once lined, the basket should be partially filled with compost (again definitely not garden soil) ready to receive plants. As you fill, moisten the compost and pack it in quite firmly and in the top make a 'dished' shape to prevent flooding over the sides when the basket is watered.

Plants should be positioned both in the top of the basket and poked through the sides so that a complete covering of cascading foliage and flowers will be achieved. For the top, a plant of upright habit could be chosen, but do make sure it is low growing or it will become tangled in the suspending wires or damaged in the wind. A low-growing geranium would be fine, and you can always pinch out the top to encourage bushy rather than upright growth.

Baskets can look equally stunning furnished with one single type of plant or a mixture – perhaps a colour theme of pink and white, mauve and blue or reds and oranges. Summer-flowering trailing plants that can be used to good effect include fuchsias, ivy-leaf geranium, lobelia and trailing nasturtium; also useful would be ivy; petunias and busy lizzies, which hang nicely if not exactly trailing; sweet alyssum; heliotrope; verbena and *Phlox drummondii*.

Hanging baskets need not be useful only in summer months. In the autumn they should be emptied and cleaned, but could then be planted up again for winter with hardy plants; these could even remain as a permanent feature of a small group of baskets which would make a framework of your collection. Suitable plants include ivy again, which can be kept over from summer displays (once greenhouse grown plants have been out for a whole spring and summer they should be quite hardy) and also the lovely creeping jenny (*Lysimachia nummularia*) – a British wild plant with showy yellow flowers which are often fragrant.

Other hardy plants for baskets are the lovely little wall plant *Campanula muralis*; the blue periwinkle *Vinca minor* and *Nepeta hederacea*. Spring flowering bulbs like miniature narcissus, crocuses, snowdrops and scilla could also make a good display early in the year.

Hanging baskets are exposed to sun and wind all round, so they tend to dry out rather quickly, especially in summer. Frequent watering is therefore essential, and indeed it is virtually impossible to overwater. Access could be a problem and it might be practical to have a small ladder on hand so that you can water easily into the top of the basket – this should be done at least once a day. You can also obtain a special attachment for watering cans which makes a form of spout extension and could be useful.

Add a dilute liquid fertilizer once a week or make use of slow-release fertilizer pellets to save a few more trips up and down the ladder! Dead flower heads should be picked off as often as possible to keep the plants looking their best. Even lobelia is better for this although it is a fiddly job best done with a pair of nail scissors.

Whether you choose for your garden hanging baskets, a mass of exuberantly planted pots or a few well-chosen specimens – or a combination of all three; whether you have sprawling rural acres or a tiny corner of the city, the chances are that you will find container gardening an enjoyable form of growing. Dedicated gardeners may become thoroughly absorbed and boldly experimental, whilst those less committed will probably be continually grateful for plants that seem to provide quick, impressive effect with so little care and attention!

A simple trellis and pergola
transformed by hanging
baskets and wall pots.

Chapter eleven
Plants for containers

An easy-reference summary of plants recommended in the book as being particularly suitable for container gardening

Weeping trees

Betula pendula 'Youngii'
Cotoneaster 'Hybridus Pendulus'
Fagus sylvatica 'Purpurea Pendula'
Ilex aquifolium 'Pendula'
Prunus 'Cheal's Weeping'
Salix caprea 'Pendula'

Shrubs

Acer palmatum
Acer palmatum 'atropurpureum'
Acer palmatum 'Dissectum'
Acer palmatum 'Dissectum
    Atropurpureum'
Aralia elata
Arundinaria viridistriata
Astelia
Buxus sempervirens
Camellias in variety
Cordyline australis
Corylus avellana 'Contorta'
Fatsia japonica
Hydrangea (mophead and lacecap
    types)

Laurus nobilis
Phormium tenax in variety
Rhododendron and Azalea in variety
Roses in variety
Yucca filamentosa

Conifers

Cedrus atlantica glauca
Cedrus deodara
Chamaecyparis lawsoniana
    'Columnaris Glauca'
Juniperus virginiana 'Skyrocket'
Picea glauca 'Albertiana Conica'
Pinus mugo 'Humpy'
Pinus mugo 'Mops'
Pinus mugo 'Ophir'
Thuja occidentalis 'Smaragd'

Climbers

Ampelopsis brevipedunculata
    'Elegans'
Clematis in variety
Fremontodendron californicum
    'Californian Glory'

123

Plants for Containers

Hedera canariensis
Hedera helix in variety
Roses – climbers and ramblers in
    variety
Wisteria sinensis

Perennial plants

Agapanthus Headbourne Hybrids
Astilbe
Campanula lactiflora in variety
Ferns, especially
    Asplenium scolopendrium
    Athyrium filix-femina
    Dryopteris filix-mas
    Matteuccia struthiopteris
Hemerocallis in variety
Hosta in variety

Bulbs

Anemone de Caen
Anemone St Brigid
Colchicum species and hybrids
Crocus
Cyclamen
Erythronium dens-canis
Fritillaria imperialis
Galanthus
Hyacinth
Iris varieties
Lilium species and hybrids
Muscari
Narcissus cyclamineum in variety
Narcissus jonquilla
Narcissus minnow
Narcissus triandrus albus
Scilla
Tulipa species
Tulipa kaufmanniana hybrids
Tulipa fosteriana hybrids

Tulipa greigii hybrids
Single early tulips
Double early tulips

Annuals and seasonal flowers

Alyssum
Antirrhinum
Begonia semperflorens
Calendula
Candytuft
Fuchsia in variety
Geranium (zonal pelargonium)
Lobelia
Mesembryanthemum
Nasturtium
Nemesia
Pansies
Petunia
Phlox drummondii
Pinks (annual varieties)
Polyanthus
Scabious
Wallflower

Seasonal climbers

Canary creeper
Cobaea scandens
Morning glory
Nasturtium – traling varieties
Sweet peas

Herbs

Chervil
Chives
Fennel
Mint in variety
Parsley
Rosemary
Rue
Sage
Savory
Tarragon
Thyme in variety

Vegetables

Aubergine
Pepper
Tomato
Runner bean

Fruit

Dwarf apple and plum
Strawberry

Acknowledgements

For their help in making this book possible we would like to thank:
Mr Leonard van Geest, Chris Chew and all at Geest Horticulture, Spalding who have generously supported us with the supply of plants, without which it would not have been possible to obtain many of the photographs.

Duncan & Davies of Highleigh, Chichester for supplying plants from New Zealand and Brian Hamilton for Chinese and terracotta pots.

Also thanks to Carol Smith, Derek Goard and Heather Angel, to Diane Drummond and to Connie Austen Smith, our editor.

Picture Acknowledgements

Reference for illustrations include pots by Haddonstone, Olive Tree Trading and E.H. Brannam. Photograph P. 86 garden by Cramphorn; P. 122 garden by Erin Marketing/British Bedding Plant Association. Several photographs show Halifax Building Society Courtyard Garden, Chelsea Show. Heather Angel P. 15, 23, 39, 42, 47, 71, 106 (bottom), 111, P. 14 Reproduced by courtesy of the Trustees, The National Gallery, London. P. 10–11, 126 Reproduced by courtesy of The Tate Gallery, London. All other photographs by Derek Goard.

125

'Gardening' by N. Gontcharova

Index

Acer palmatum 100, 123;
  'Atropurpureum' 45, 123;
  'Dissectum' 33, 45, 123;
  'Dissectum Atropurpureum' 45,
  123. *See also* Japanese maple
Agapanthus Headbourne Hybrids
  61, 100, 124
Ageratum 104
Allium cyaneum 73. *See also* Chinese
  garlic
Alpine gentian 73
Alyssum 66, 104, 120, 124. *See
  also* Sweet alyssum
Ampelopsis brevipedunculata 'Elegans'
  57, 104, 123
Anemone 65; de Caen 124;
  'St Brigid' 124
Antennaria dioica 'Minima' 73
Antirrhinum 66, 124
Apple (dwarf) 44, 125
Aralia elata 44, 123. *See also*
  Japanese angelica
Armeria caespitosa 73. *See also*
  Miniature thrift
Arundinaria viridistriata 52, 100,
  123. *See also* Bamboo
Asplenium scolopendrium 58, 124.
  See also Hart's tongue fern
Astelia 52, 60, 123
Astilbe 58, 100, 105, 124;
  'Amethyst' 60; 'Fanal' 60; 'White
  Gloria' 60
Athyrium filix-femina 58, 124. *See
  also* Lady fern
Aubergine 20, 69, 125
Azalea 20, 32, 123

Bamboo 52, 100, 123. *See also
  Arundinaria viridistriata*
Bay 45, 48, 90, 101, 123. *See also
  Laurus nobilis*
Begonia 66; *B. semperflorens* 66,
  124
Betula pendula 'Youngii' 41, 123.
  See also Young's weeping birch
Bonsai 96
Box 48, 90, 101, 123. *See also
  Buxus sempervirens*
Busy lizzie 102, 112, 117, 120
Buxus sempervirens 48, 90, 101,
  123 *See also* Box

Calendula 20, 66, 102, 124. *See
  also* Pot marigold
Camellia 32, 49–50, 102, 105, 123
Campanula: dwarf 73; *C. lactiflora*
  61, 124; *C. muralis* 121

Canary creeper 66, 90, 92, 102,
  125
Candytuft 66
Cedrus atlantica glauca 54, 123;
  C. deodara 54, 100, 123
Cellular fibre planters 18, 20
Cerise 92
Chamaecyparis lawsoniana
  'Columnaris Glauca' 73, 123
Chervil 68, 125
Chimney pots as containers 28
Chinese garlic 73. *See also Allium
  cyaneum*
Chinese glazed earthenware
  containers 22, 48–9, 80
Chionodoxa luciliae 65
Chives 68, 125
Chlorophytum 20, 104. *See also*
  Spider plant
Chrysanthemum frutescens 85, 101
Clay pots 20, 58
Clematis: *C. montana* 56, 90, 105,
  123
Climbing rose 57, 90; 'Danse de
  Feu' 57; 'Gloire de Dijon' 57;
  'Golden Showers' 57; 'Guinee'
  57; 'Madame Alfred Carriere' 57;
  'Madame Gregoire Stachelin' 57
Cobaea scandens 66, 125
Colchicum 65, 124
Coleus 20, 66, 102
Compost: for alpines 70–2; for
  containers 31–2
Conifers generally 37
Convolvulus 92
Cordyline 37, 52, 100–101;
  C. australis 123
Corkscrew hazel 38, 45, 100, 123.
  See also Corylus avellana
  'Contorta'
Cotoneaster 'Hybridus Pendulus' 41,
  123
Creeping jenny 120. *See also
  Lysimachia nummularia*
Crocus 64–5, 73, 104, 113, 121,
  124
Crown imperial 22, 38, 65, 92,
  104, 124. *See also Fritillaria
  imperialis*
Cyclamen coum 64–5, 105, 124

Daffodil 90
Day lily 60, 100, 124. *See also*
  Hemerocallis
Dog's tooth violet 124. *See also
  Erythronium dens-canis*
Dryopteris filix-mas 58, 124. *See also*

Male fern
Dwarf apple 44, 125
Dwarf conifers 73. *See also* varieties
  of Chamaecyparis, Juniperus,
  Picea, Pinus, Taxus
Dwarf mountain forget-me-not 73
Dwarf plum 44, 125
Dwarf water lily 77. *See also
  Nymphaea pygmaea*

Erythronium dens-canis 124. *See also*
  Dog's tooth violet

Fagus sylvatica 'Purpurea Pendula'
  41, 123
Fatsia japonica 38, 52, 100, 105,
  123
Feeding container plants 33, 35
Fennel 68, 125
Ferns 33. *See also Asplenium
  scolopendrium* (Hart's tongue fern)
  58, 124; *Athyrium filix – femina*
  (Lady fern) 58, 124; *Dryopteris
  filix-mas* (Male fern) 58, 124;
  Matteuccia struthiopteris (Ostrich
  feather fern) 58, 124
Foxglove 61
Fremontodendron californicum
  'Californian Glory' 57, 123
Fritillaria imperialis 22, 38, 65, 92,
  104, 124. *See also* Crown
  imperial
Fuchsia 20, 37, 49, 66, 85, 90,
  92–3, 100–101, 104, 120, 124

Galanthus 65, 124
Geranium 20, 36, 52, 66, 85, 90,
  100–102, 104, 112, 120, 124
Grape hyacinth 73

Harry Lauder's walking stick 38,
  45, 100, 123. *See also Corylus
  avellana* 'Contorta'
Hart's tongue fern 58, 124. *See also
  Asplenium scolopendrium*
Heather 112
Hedera canariensis 124
Hedera helix 38, 49, 56, 85, 90,
  100, 104–5, 112, 120, 124;
  'Buttercup' 104. *See also* Ivy
Helichrysum 66, 90
Heliotrope 120
Hemerocallis 60, 100, 124. *See also*
  Day lily
Hosta 33, 35, 37, 58, 60–1, 81, 92,
  105, 124; *H. fortunei* 58;
  H. fortunei 'Aurea Marginata' 58;

Index

H. fortunei 'Picta' 58; *H. sieboldiana glauca* 58
Holly 44
Houseleek 73. *See also* Sempervivum
Hyacinth 64–5, 104–5, 112, 124
Hydrangea 22, 25, 37, 50, 92, 101, 123

Ihsing pottery 22
Ilex aquifolium 'Pendula' 44, 123
Ipomea 66, 104, 125. *See also* Morning glory
Iris (miniature) 64, 73, 124; *I. danfordiae* 65, 104; *I. reticulata* 65, 105
Ivy 38, 49, 56, 85, 90, 100, 104–5, 112, 120, 124. *See also* Hedera helix

Japanese angelica 44, 123. *See also* Aralia elata
Japanese maple 35, 45, 100, 123. *See also* Acer palmatum
Jardiniere 24
Juniperus communis 'Compressa' 73. *See also* Miniature Irish juniper
Juniperus virginiana 'Skyrocket' 53, 123

Kilmarnock willow 40–1, 100, 123. *See also* Salix caprea 'Pendula'

Lady fern 58, 124. *See also* Athyrium filix-femina
Laurus nobilis 45, 48, 90, 101, 123. *See also* Bay
Lead containers 25
Lighting effects 101
Lilium 22, 38, 65, 90, 124
Lobelia 66, 90, 104, 116, 120, 124
Lysimachia nummularia 120. *See also* Creeping jenny

Male fern 58, 124. *See also* Dryopteris filix-mas
Marble containers 25
Matteuccia struthiopteris 58, 124. *See also* Ostrich feather fern
Mesembryanthemum 66, 124
Miniature Irish juniper 73. *See also* Juniperus communis 'Compressa'
Miniature *Narcissus* 'Tete-a-Tete' 73
Miniature thrift 73. *See also* Armeria caesiptosa
Mint 68, 125
Morning glory 66, 104, 125. *See also* Ipomea
Mountain pine 54, 123. *See also* Pinus mugo
Moving container plants 35
Muscari 44, 65, 105, 124
Myosotis rupicola 73

Narcissus 22, 38, 64, 104, 112, 120, 124: *N. cyclamineum* 65, 124; *N. jonquilla* 65, 124; *N. minnow* 65, 124; 'Tete-a-Tete' 73; *N. triandrus albus* 65, 124
Nasturtium 66, 92, 102, 120, 124–5
Nemesia 66, 124
Nepeta hederacea 121
New Zealand flax 37, 52, 92, 123. *See also* Phormium tenax
Nicotiana 104
Nymphaea pygmaea 77. *See also* Dwarf water lily

Ornamental flowering cherry 44, 123. *See also* Prunus 'Cheal's Weeping'
Ostrich feather fern 58, 124. *See also* Matteuccia struthiopteris

Pansy 66, 85, 113, 124
Parsley 68, 125
Pepper 20, 69, 125
Pergola 54, 56–7, 90, 118
Periwinkle 121. *See also* Vinca minor
Petunia 20, 66, 85, 92, 100, 104, 112, 120, 124
Phlox: *P. douglasii* 'Red Admiral' 73; *P. douglasii rosea* 73; *P. douglasii* 'Waterloo' 73; *P. drummondii* 66, 120, 124
Phormium tenax 37, 52, 92, 123; dwarf varieties 73; 'Sundowner' 52; 'Yellow Wave' 52, 92. *See also* New Zealand flax
Picea glauca 'Albertiana Conica' 53–4, 123
Pink 66, 124
Pinus mugo: dwarf varieties 73; 'Humpy' 54, 123; 'Mops' 54, 123; 'Ophir' 54, 123. *See also* Mountain pine
Polyanthus 20, 66, 85, 112–13, 124
Pot marigold 22, 66, 102, 124. *See also* Calendula
Prunus 'Cheal's Weeping' 44, 123. *See also* Ornamental flowering cherry

Raoulia australis 73
Rhododendron 25, 32, 37, 49, 102, 123; dwarf 76
Rosemary 68, 125
Rose 50, 57, 101, 123, 124
Rock garden pink 73
Rock primulas 73
Rue 68, 125
Runner beans 69, 125

Sage 68, 104, 125
Salix caprea 'Pendula' 40–1, 100,

123. *See also* Kilmarnock willow
Savory 68, 125
Saxifraga aizoon balderis 73; 'Kabschia' types 73
Scabious 124
Scilla 44, 65, 105, 121, 124
Sempervivum 73. *See also* Houseleek
Silene acaulis 73
Silver-leaf 20, 66, 104
Sisyrinchium brachypus 73
Snowdrop 64, 105, 113, 121
Spider plant 20, 104. *See also* Chlorophytum
Sternbergia 65
Stone containers 24–5, 48–9
Strawberry 69, 125
Sweet alyssum 66, 104, 120, 124
Sweet peas 66, 92, 104, 125
Sweet scabious 66

Tarragon 68, 125
Taxus, dwarf varieties 73
Terracotta pots 21, 48, 52, 80
Thrift (miniature) 73. *See also* Armeria caespitosa
Thuja occidentalis 'Smaragd' 53, 123
Thymus 'Silver Queen' 104–5
Thyme 68, 73, 84, 104, 112, 125
Tomato 20, 69, 125
Tulip 20, 38, 44, 64–5, 90, 104, 116, 124: *T. fosteriana* 65, 124; *T. greigii* 65, 124; *T. kaufmanniana* 65, 124; *T. kaufmanniana* 'Heart's Delight' 105; *T. praestans* 65; *T. praestans* 'Fusilier' 104; *T. tarda* 65

Verbena 120
Versailles tubs 24, 102
Vinca minor 121. *See also* Periwinkle
Viola 66

Wallflower 66, 124
Water hyacinth 77
Water lettuce 77
Water lily (dwarf) 77. *See also* Nymphaea pygmaea
Water moss 77
Water soldier 77
Watering container plants 33
Wisteria sinensis 56, 57, 90, 123
Wooden containers 24, 48–9, 54

Young's weeping birch 41, 123. *See also* Betula pendula 'Youngii'
Yucca filamentosa 52, 92, 100–101, 123

Zinnia 66
Zonal pelargonium 20, 36, 52, 66, 85, 90, 100–102, 104, 112, 120, 124. *See also* Geranium